Hanging on in there

A study of inter-agency work to prevent school exclusion in three local authorities

Gwynedd Lloyd, Joan Stead and Andrew Kendrick

JR
JOSEPH
ROWNTREE
FOUNDATION

NATIONAL
CHILDREN'S
BUREAU

making a difference

The National Children's Bureau promotes the interests and well-being of all children and young people across every aspect of their lives. NCB advocates the participation of children and young people in all matters affecting them. NCB challenges disadvantage in childhood.

NCB achieves its mission by
- ensuring the views of children and young people are listened to and taken into account at all times
- playing an active role in policy development and advocacy
- undertaking high quality research and work from an evidence based perspective
- promoting multidisciplinary, cross-agency partnerships
- identifying, developing and promoting good practice
- disseminating information to professionals, policy makers, parents and children and young people

NCB has adopted and works within the UN Convention on the Rights of the Child.

Several Councils and Fora are based at NCB and contribute significantly to the breadth of its influence. It also works in partnership with Children in Scotland and Children in Wales and other voluntary organisations concerned for children and their families.

The Joseph Rowntree Foundation has supported this project as part of its programme of research and innovative development projects, which it hopes will be of value to policy makers and practitioners.

The views expressed in this book are those of the authors and not necessarily those of the National Children's Bureau or the Joseph Rowntree Foundation.

Published by National Children's Bureau Enterprises Ltd, the trading company for the National Children's Bureau, Registered Charity number 258825. 8 Wakley Street, London EC1V 7QE. Tel: 020 7843 6000

© National Children's Bureau and Joseph Rowntree Foundation, 2001
Published 2001

ISBN 1 900990 68 7

British Library Cataloguing in Publication Data
A catalogue record for this book is available from the British Library

Designed and typeset by Jeff Teader
Printed and bound by Page Bros, Norwich

Contents

List of tables and figures

Acknowledgements

The research team would like to thank all the young people, their parents/ guardians, school staff and professionals for taking part in the research, and the key personnel in the three local authorities who collaborated with us.

We particularly wish to thank our advisory group, Malcolm Hill, Bernadette Docherty, Bill Maxwell, Alan Dyson, Paul Millsop, Maria Lucia Macconnachie and Hamish MacPhee, for their supportive criticism; also Dorothy Bruce, Lesley Scullion, Pam Henderson, Pauline Clark and Barry Wilford. We especially wish to thank Charlie Lloyd of the Joseph Rowntree Foundation for his support and guidance.

Glossary

Behaviour support teachers. The development of behaviour support services in schools emphasises cooperative working with teachers to support or change their classroom management. Behaviour support also involves contact with individual pupils. A school may have designated permanent behaviour support teachers, or they may be peripatetic/part time. However, the role of behaviour support is not formalised in many schools and may be part of learning support.

Children's Hearing System. A welfare based system providing a structure of intervention and support for children who are considered to require compulsory measures of care and/or control. The Hearings offer a formal process in an informal setting, where parents and children are present. Decisions are made by a small panel of lay people who are trained part-time volunteers (see Reporter below).

Education Welfare Officer. Previously referred to as Attendance Officer.

Exclusion from school. In Scotland there are two categories of disciplinary exclusion from school – 'temporary exclusion' for a limited period of time and 'exclusion/removed from the register'. There is no category of 'permanent exclusion' as there is in England.

Guidance teachers. Promoted teachers in secondary schools throughout Scotland who have specific responsibility for the personal, academic and vocational welfare of pupils. Every pupil is allocated a guidance teacher. The number and deployment of these posts varies from school to school. Very few posts are full time, most combine subject teaching with a number of hours 'non-teaching' support time.

Learning Support Teacher. Learning Support has five roles in relation to the broad based and special educational needs of pupils (including those with a Record of Needs, see below). These roles are in relation to (1) direct teaching; (2) cooperative teaching in class; (3) consultancy to class; (4) liaison with relevant professionals; (5) staff development.

Record of Needs. Similar to 'Statement' in England – a formalised plan for the special educational needs of a particular pupil.

Reporter. The Reporter, often a qualified solicitor, acts as gatekeeper to the Children's Hearing System. The Reporter would receive, assess evidence and prioritise (or dismiss) referrals to the Children's Hearing and would provide support and advice to the lay members (the Panel) who make decisions about intervention (see Children's Hearing System above).

Scottish Executive. Refers to the Scottish government post devolution. The Scottish Parliament has devolved powers for education, health, and social welfare, amongst others.

(S)EBD. Refers to social, emotional, behavioural difficulties and is the term used in Scotland. In England the term does not include the prefix social (S).

Youth Strategy. A term used to denote both a strategy of inter-agency work with young people and specific initiatives.

1. Introduction

This report discusses the findings of a study, funded by the Joseph Rowntree Foundation, conducted from February 2000 to April 2001. The study investigated inter-agency initiatives in relation to the prevention of school exclusion. It explored issues of effectiveness in terms of outcomes for young people; young people's, and their parents', perceptions of success; and the effectiveness of involved professionals.

Government policies at Westminster and those of the devolved Scottish Executive emphasise social justice and inclusion. Disciplinary exclusion from school is viewed as part of the wider problem of social exclusion and has been targeted for specific action. Education authorities and schools are expected to reduce their current levels of exclusion from school. In Scotland the Executive aims to reduce by a third the days lost through exclusion and truancy. However, recent education legislation and guidance in Scotland, as in the rest of Britain, still allows for both disciplinary exclusion and for special out of school placement of pupils whose behaviour is considered to be unacceptable, either in terms of the welfare of the individual pupil and/or the welfare of the wider school community. Most education authorities in Scotland, while continuing to use exclusion, have policies, and in some cases long established procedures, designed to reduce exclusion and to encourage more effective inter-agency working to support children and young people in their family and in their local school.

The recent government emphasis on 'joined-up working' recognises that interrelated issues and problems require interrelated assessment, planning and practice to achieve effective solutions. The moral and strategic arguments for collaboration are powerful, especially in relation to the welfare and best interests of children, with advocacy and multi-agency working becoming an integral part of much legislation, policy and practice over the last ten years. In particular, the Children Act 1989 and the Children (Scotland) Act 1995 now provide comprehensive mandates for the coordination of planning for local services for children, giving political priority to inter-agency collaboration. In Scotland, as in other parts of the UK, the issue of disciplinary exclusion from school is increasingly being discussed as part of the wider issues of social exclusion and inclusion. Offending, family conflict and school related problems are seen as closely interrelated and the dominant issues leading to referral to social work departments; other research has shown that education personnel have acknowledged and valued the potential contribution of a social work approach to maintaining children in school (Triseliotis and others, 1995).

Inter-agency working is, however, not easy. For example, as part of the government's Social Inclusion Strategy, the 'Making it Happen Strategy Action Team' was set up 'to make recommendations about ways of overcoming professional, organisational and cultural barriers to promoting social inclusion'. In its report it identifies three types of barriers to effective working:

> **Structural and Functional Barriers** – fragmentation of public services because of range of organisations involved in their delivery; agencies structured around the services to be delivered rather than the areas or groups served.
> **Process Barriers** – inflexibilities caused by the financial procedures of agencies; the processes of some central government funding which encourages short-termism and forced partnerships.
> **Cultural Barriers** – each profession, each organisation can have their own way of doing things and their own sometimes ill-informed views of the other organisations and professions with which they deal. *(Scottish Executive, 1999)*

Much of the literature describes education and social work as having different norms, dialects and missions which promote conflict, and Parsons (1999) adds to this list different training, hierarchies, pay scales, funding and physical locations as challenges for successful inter-agency working. The different perspectives are further illustrated by Triseliotis and others (1995) (writing from a social work perspective) who take a conciliatory view on inter-agency relations, mentioning the need for communication between agencies to be constructive and empathetic. Research on Youth Strategies in Scotland identified the increased participation of young people and parents in joint education and social work meetings as a positive result of inter-agency work (Kendrick, 1995). This contrasts with other research which highlights parents' feelings of powerlessness to influence the process of school exclusion (Cohen and others, 1994).

What is inter-agency work?

This whole area has often been described as a 'terminological quagmire', so developing clarity within our thinking has been important. For example, inter-agency is sometimes used to denote working between only two agencies, but others use it to refer to a range of agencies working together (Wilson and Pirrie, 2000; Arblaster and others, 1999). In this study we use the following definitions. They have been developed through the structuring and analysing of our data and after consideration of other definitions in the research literature. Equally, the development of models of different kinds of working and the situations to which they are appropriate may be helpful to policy makers and practitioners rather than simple exhortations to do it (Leathard, 1994).

Definitions

Inter-agency working means when more than one agency work together in a *planned and formal* way, rather than simply through informal networking (although a history of the latter may, as we shall argue, provide a helpful support for the former). This can be at the level of local authority policy making or at the level of local agencies.

Joined-up means deliberately conceptualised and coordinated planning and working which takes account of different policies and varying agency practices and values. This can refer to thinking or to practice or policy development. This, as we shall argue later, is central to the social inclusion policies of both the Scottish Executive and the Westminster governments.

Joint working is when professionals from more than one agency work directly together on a project, for example in teachers and social work staff offering joint group work. School Based Inter-agency Meetings may involve *joint* planning, which reflects *joined-up* thinking.

Multi-agency working involves more than one agency working with a young person, with a family or on a project (but *not necessarily jointly*). It may be *concurrent* when two different agencies are working at the same time with a young person. This could happen as a result of *joint planning* which has happened in an inter-agency meeting or it could be as the consequence of a lack of effective inter-agency communication. Equally, it may be *sequential*, where different agencies are involved with a young person at different times, sometimes as a planned sequence or sometimes for historical or resource reasons.

Single agency working where only one agency is involved may still be the consequence of inter-agency decision making and therefore may be part of a joined-up plan.

Multi-professional working refers to the working together of staff with different professional backgrounds and training. Thus some of the individual projects in this study may be *inter-agency*, in that their policy context involves more than one agency and they may be funded by more than one local authority budget. They may do joined-up working with others in meetings. They may do joint work, for example with teachers from local schools, and they usually were staffed by a multi-disciplinary team.

Inter-agency communication refers to information sharing – formal and informal – between agencies, written or oral.

Effectiveness

There is no magic formula of successful inter-agency working, and no way of clearly establishing that any change or improvement would not have happened anyway, without any intervention. Assessing effectiveness involves making judgements about the outcomes of professional activities (Hill, 1999). Determining the effectiveness of a professional activity often does not adequately take into account client/stakeholder perspectives. Until recently the views of young people and their parents were not often sought. Any attempt at objectively defining effectiveness also raises issues about the heterogeneity of any group or categorisation.

Perceptions of success/effectiveness depends on the definition of the problem, moving us again into the vexed question around exclusion – whose problems are we discussing? Are they the management problems of schools and teachers or are they the young people's problems? If this project had been focusing on how schools supported vulnerable young people at risk of social exclusion, the question would be easier to explore. The context of exclusion means that effectiveness becomes involved with an apparently easy to measure indicator, but one which may be affected as much by a range of variables within and to do with the school and how it works, as it is by the actions of an individual pupil (Parsons, 1999; Munn and others, 2000).

One clear factor, however, in understanding exclusion rates is the level of support provided to young people to enable them to avoid exclusion. This study has explored how the support that was provided in the six case study schools was viewed by its recipients and by those providing the support. Despite the complexity of issues affecting young people it was possible to identify some characteristics of effective helping and to explore the varying notions of what appeared to be success to all participants. Notions of success ranged from the short term, for example, exclusions from school, to longer-term thinking about adult futures.

Outline of study

Our research design and methodology was collaboratively developed as part of our partnership with three participating Scottish Local Authorities, all of whom had a history of inter-agency working. Our questions were:

What is the context in which inter-agency initiatives have developed in three Scottish authorities with regard to the prevention of disciplinary exclusion from secondary schools?

How effective are inter-agency initiatives in relation to the prevention of school exclusion in three Scottish authorities?

What are stakeholders' perceptions of inter-agency initiatives?

What are the factors which facilitate or inhibit the development and/or effectiveness of such provision?

We undertook policy and documentary analysis at three levels: local authority, schools, and files of individual professionals (e.g. school files and social work files). We interviewed 18 key personnel with strategic responsibilities. Towards the end of the research focus groups were held with a wide range of policy makers and managers to discuss preliminary findings, and clarify structural and policy issues.

Key to inter-agency working in each local authority was the long established School Based Inter-agency Meeting. Each local authority identified two secondary schools for the research and we observed two meetings in each school and examined, where possible, the minutes of previous meetings.

We interviewed 30 young people and 25 parents. We interviewed 34 school staff and 43 other professionals and asked specific questions relating to the young person with whom they were involved, and more general questions relating to School Based Inter-agency Meetings and wider aspects of inter-agency working.

The story told in this report is about the delivery of policy initiatives involving collaboration at different levels. Arblaster and colleagues (1999) identify four levels of collaboration: the strategic; the locality; the client group; and individual client services. The client group in our research is young people involved in disciplinary exclusion in school. This report refers to three levels of collaboration: corporate polices at the strategic level and structures of the three local authorities; systems for decision making at the school and neighbourhood level; direct services for young people.

The School Based Inter-agency Meetings evolved in a national context of inter-agency working. In Chapter 2 we provide an overview of the policy context in Scotland, making some broad comparisons with England. In Chapter 3 we outline characteristics of the local authorities, schools and pupils in the research. Chapter 4 focuses on the School Based Inter-agency Meetings, the differences, similarities, advantages and disadvantages. Chapter 5 discusses the effectiveness of direct inter-agency work with young people. Chapter 6 draws together the key findings and some issues raised.

All names of local authorities, schools and young people are pseudonyms but when 'pen pictures' are used they are of real pupils, not composites.

2. Policy context

In this chapter we outline the Scottish policy context and the history of inter-agency working in relation to disciplinary exclusion from school. We relate this to other key aspects, including policy and legislation, on the social welfare of children and young people, and on special education needs.

The principle of inter-agency working

Joint working between social work, education and other agencies has a long history in Scotland. In 1964 the Report of the Kilbrandon Committee proposed that children and young people in difficulty should be dealt with in 'social education departments' managing both education and social services in an integrated way (Scottish Office, 1964; Schaffer, 1992; Kendrick and others, 1995). While the 'social education departments' were never established, collaborative responses have been formalised in 'youth strategies' in Scotland since the early 1980s (Pickles, 1992; Kendrick and others, 1995). Some youth strategies were characterised by a broad, community development approach, others emphasise keeping children out of residential education. The intention was to reduce the need for formal intervention in the lives of young people by increasing the range of informal, non-statutorily based, support. Youth strategies also often involved the development of jointly funded education and social work provision for young people, sometimes to provide after school groupwork or individual support and sometimes to offer short-term or part-time education for young people facing difficulties at school. As in England, this kind of initiative was often seen to be part of a range of provision described as intermediate treatment.

Inter-agency School Based Meetings were developed which brought together representatives from school guidance (in Scottish secondary schools guidance teachers are part subject teacher and part pastoral care), learning support, school health, educational psychology, the social work department, the community education department and often neighbourhood based voluntary sector projects, to develop school-wide strategies and to consider cases of young people having difficulties in school and at risk of school exclusion.

The development of Youth Strategies in Scotland was influenced by the uniqueness of the Scottish Children's Hearing system, one aspect of the Kilbrandon Report which was implemented, which is a welfare-based approach to juvenile justice and to responding to children and young people at risk or in trouble. The Hearing system is based on decision making by a number of lay people (volunteers from the community) who do not have vested interests in any one of the services, therefore responding primarily (in theory at least) to the best interests of the young person concerned. Although decisions are inevitably influenced by departmental recommendations and resources, Children's Hearings encourage inter-professional discussion and collaboration.

In 1996 local Government reorganisation in Scotland led to the creation of 32 unified local authorities which took over the responsibilities of the 12 regional and 53 district local authorities. Although there have been concerns regarding the implications of this for the provision of specialised services and inter-agency working, it has provided opportunities for the smaller local authorities to provide at least the possibility of closer relations between departments and an ability to focus more closely on the problems of their areas at the local level (Kendrick and others, 1996).

Continuing emphasis on the principle of inter-agency working

The principle of inter-agency work has been central to various legal and policy documents since the mid-1990s. In 1993, based on eight principles incorporating the philosophy of the United Nations Convention on the Rights of the Child, the White Paper *Scotland's Children* (Scottish Office, 1993) set out recommendations for changes in child care law and practice. The last of the eight principles was that 'any intervention in the life of a child, including the provision of supportive services, should be based on collaboration between all the relevant agencies'. Children are entitled to expect good education and health care and they have the right to expect that professionals from the different agencies will collaborate in a child-centred way (Scottish Office, 1993, pp. 6–7). This principle was taken forward in the Children (Scotland) Act 1995 with a statutory duty for local authorities to produce and publish Children's Services Plans in consultation with health agencies, voluntary organisations, representatives of the Children's Hearing system, and housing agencies. The legislation emphasised the 'corporate responsibility' of the local authority.

The Executive's social inclusion strategy includes funding for a major pilot programme of 'New Community Schools' (Scottish Executive, 1998). Drawing on the Full Service School concept from the USA, New Community Schools will, 'make integrated provision of school education, family support and health education and promotion services' and 'have clear management arrangements for the integrated management of these services'. Although none of the schools in this study were New Community Schools this policy direction is influential in current thinking in education.

Exclusion from school in Scotland

Concern over disciplinary exclusion from school is common across Britain but there are several key differences in the legislation and guidance on exclusion in England and Scotland (Munn and others, 2000). In England there is a stipulated length of fixed term exclusions and a restriction of parental rights to choose a school if their child has been excluded more than once. The length of an exclusion in Scotland is a matter for the education authority to decide, and this decision is mainly devolved to head teachers. There are no fixed terms specified in national guidance, although individual education authorities or schools may operate an informal tariff system. The law in Scotland does not use the terms temporary and permanent exclusion but, according to the national guidance, distinguishes between 'temporary exclusion' and 'exclusion/removed from the register' (Scottish Office, 1998a). Grounds of exclusion are that the pupil's continued attendance at school is seriously detrimental to order and discipline and to the educational well-being of fellow pupils or that the parent of the pupil refuses or fails to comply, or to allow the pupil to comply, with the rules, regulations or disciplinary requirements of the school. Parents may appeal to an appeals committee set up by the local authority and thereafter to the sheriff court (rather than as in England to a committee of school governors, and then judicial review). The national guidance emphasises inclusion and the use of exclusion as a last resort. The right of the pupil facing exclusion to have their views heard is emphasised, although not always observed.

Comparisons of number or rate of exclusion between Scotland and England are difficult as there are different ways of describing exclusion and of collecting data. In both systems there have been questions about the validity of some statistics, as a result of both deliberate and fortuitous inaccuracies in the data gathered from schools. Recent Scottish Executive statistics allow for more comparison, suggesting that about three times as many pupils are permanently excluded in England as removed from the register in Scotland (Scottish Executive, 2001a). There have been suggestions in the literature that children are not permanently excluded from school in Scotland. This is only the case in that they are not labelled in this way – there are still excluded/removed from the register children with no full-time educational placement.

Anomalies, misunderstandings and varying levels of honesty at school level in recording exclusion does mean that it is difficult to make comparisons between local authorities. We also know from research that schools may exclude informally or use other strategies to remove pupils (Munn and others, 2000). However the statistics do suggest quite substantial differences both between schools and between local authorities in both the rate of exclusion and the way it is used. Total numbers of pupils excluded in Scotland in 1999/2000 (temporarily or removed from the register) show a range from 55 pupils per 1,000 in the City of Glasgow to 1 per 1,000 in the Shetland Islands. The three local authorities studied in this project had varying rates of exclusion, the highest rate being Douglasshire Council with 61 instances of exclusions per 1,000 pupils, involving 33 pupils per 1,000. Wallace City Council was recorded as having 36 instances of exclusion per 1,000, involving 21 pupils per 1,000 and Glenmore Council with 16 instances per 1,000, involving 10 pupils per 1,000.

Almost all exclusions were temporarily, 60 per cent of them only once and a further 20 per cent only twice. This raises questions about the use and purpose of exclusion in Scotland where earlier research indicated that some schools used exclusion as a disciplinary sanction for behaviour which may not lead to exclusion in other schools (Munn and others, 2000). The most frequently given reasons indicated on the record for exclusion were 'general or persistent disobedience in school' (23.9 per cent), followed by 'verbal abuse of members of staff' (16 per cent), then physical abuse of fellow pupils (13 per cent). Only 360 pupils were recorded as removed from the register in Scotland (Scottish Executive, 2001a).

As in England, most excluded pupils are male. In Scotland, there is little evidence of the disproportionate exclusion of young black men, reflecting the different demographic make-up of Scotland rather than indicating a more inclusive educational system. There are disproportionate rates of exclusion for children with Records of Needs, 'looked after' children and children entitled to free school meals. The variations in the number of exclusions between the three local authorities do not correspond exactly to the entitlement of free school meals (see next chapter), reinforcing the view that rates of exclusion, although reflecting the disproportionate number of pupils eligible for free school meals, also reflect other aspects of the operation of the process of exclusion in both local authorities and schools.

Given the qualifications about data gathering, rates of exclusion in Scottish schools seem lower than in some parts of Britain. Reasons for this may be partly to do with the policy context described in this chapter. Other reasons might include wider aspects of the Scottish education system, for example the political and public commitment to the model of the comprehensive school, the greater power of the local authorities to require policy compliance, and more reduced forms of devolved school management. This may also relate to the less individualistic orientation of civil society in Scotland (Paterson, 1997).

In Scotland there are no Pupil Referral Units specifically for excluded pupils, although there is a range of provision for those with 'social, emotional and behavioural difficulties' (Munn and others, 2000). As in other parts of Britain the rate of reintegration of pupils into mainstream, once they have been out for some time, is low (Lloyd and Padfield, 1996; Farrell and Tsakalidou, 1999).

Do excluded pupils have special educational needs?

Special educational provision is required, according to Scottish education law, to be made for those who have greater difficulties in learning than their peers. A child or young person has 'a "learning difficulty" if additional arrangements need to be made to enable them properly to access the curriculum' (SOEID, 1996). Difficulties in learning are defined widely and described as being caused by a variety of factors, including a child's behaviour or social and emotional development. Social, emotional and behavioural difficulties (SEBD) can be a reason for a child or young person to be considered to have special educational needs. Where such special educational needs are seen to be pronounced, specific or complex and to require continuing review, the education authority is required to open a Record of Needs. Considerable variation in levels of Recording are found within and between education authorities (Closs, 1997). This variation is most marked in relation to social, emotional and behavioural difficulties where some pupils may have Records whereas others, even many of those in full-time special educational provision, may not. There are a disproportionate number of pupils with Records of Need excluded. The relationship between exclusion, Recording and the use of special provision is complex, perhaps confused.

The recently published Report *Alternatives to school exclusion* from the Scottish HMI (2001) emphasises that most pupils who are excluded would not be considered to have social, emotional and behavioural difficulties. HMI argue that the real challenge for schools is to develop 'more effective ways of working with the small number of pupils whose challenging behaviour is not an isolated event and who can consequently find themselves excluded on a number of occasions. These pupils do have special educational needs arising from their social, emotional and behavioural difficulties' (HMI, 2001, p. 5).

The national legislative and policy context is not joined-up

Pupils who have been excluded or who are at risk of exclusion from school may be dealt with in terms of education law and procedures and/or in terms of the social welfare law and procedures of the Children (Scotland) Act 1995, including those relating to the Children's Hearing System. The procedures and the rights of children and families in each are quite different. The Children (Scotland) Act 1995 gives children and young people the right to have their views considered – this right is not specified in the educational law and procedures for the assessment of special educational needs. In Children's Hearings children and families will be present and must understand the basis on which decisions are made. The position of children and families in relation to School Based Inter-agency Meetings varies considerably.

Presuming inclusion

The recent Scottish educational legislation, the Standards in Scotland's Schools etc. Act 2000 introduces for all pupils a 'presumption of mainstream education'. The Guidance for Education Authorities on the presumption of mainstream states that 'The intention behind the new duty is to establish the right of all children and young persons to be educated along with their peers in mainstream school unless there are good reasons for not doing so.' However, the Guidance acknowledges that 'the needs of some children' may be best met through special provision if there are particular reasons why an individual child might need some small scale or highly specialised setting and second, the argument often made around exclusion, if the inclusion of one child 'may be incompatible with an education authority's duty towards all of the children in its care. Children regularly displaying severely challenging behaviour, for example, can have negative effects on the education of children around them' (Scottish Executive, 2000a).

The Act gives all children of school age the right to be provided with school education; previously parents had a duty and education authorities had a duty to provide an adequate and efficient education but children had no specified rights to receive schooling. However the possibility of disciplinary exclusion is still clearly specified.

Scottish Executive initiatives around exclusion

School exclusion and problem behaviour in school have been addressed in a number of policy and funding initiatives: Promoting Positive Discipline, the Ethos Network and the Alternatives to Exclusion Initiative (Scottish Office, 1998b; Munn and others, 2000). Multi-disciplinary and inter-agency cooperation are promoted in the guidance on Alternatives to Exclusion:

■ mechanisms for ensuring that, at an early stage, schools and other agencies inform each other about pupils in difficulty and discuss those difficulties;

■ mechanisms for coordinating a full range of appropriate assessments involving teachers and professionals from other agencies and integrating these to provide a picture of the whole child;

■ mechanisms for jointly planning, undertaking and reviewing programmes of intervention to address underlying difficulties identified;

■ joint mechanisms for the placement and review of pupils in special provision; and mechanisms to ensure appropriate collaboration between education, social work and, where appropriate, other agencies, with regard to pupils in residential provision or children who are being 'looked after' by the local authority in children's homes or other contexts. *(Scottish Office, 1998b, p. 19)*

The Alternative to Exclusion Initiative has recently been evaluated (HMI, 2001). The report was critical of the lack of systematic evaluation of outcomes in several local authorities and schools, arguing for a more rigorous approach. The funding specification for projects required 'multi-disciplinary working'. The report argues that 'establishing and maintaining multi-disciplinary teams often proved to be difficult'. Sometimes specific individuals were recruited to posts in a designated project team but these posts proved difficult to fill because of the short-term nature of the contracts. Such projects often sought support from existing agencies who found this difficult to give because of other pressures. The report suggests however that effective multi-disciplinary work could enhance the effectiveness of the support provided for pupils. But there was a recognition that the general level of joint working in authorities was not always sufficient to ensure that collaborative practices developed in the projects could be adopted more widely.

Conclusion

In this chapter we have described the history of initiatives in Scotland and their policy context. We have suggested that exclusion from school seems to be lower in Scotland than in England and that there may be a range of reasons to do with both general and specific aspects of the Scottish education and social welfare systems. Nevertheless there is concern about exclusion from school. As in England, there are calls for greater social inclusion and reduction in exclusion, but also for the right of schools to continue to exclude and for the inappropriateness of mainstream school for some pupils.

The context is complex and any account will inevitably be multi-factorial. There is a plethora of policy documents and, as in England, rapid policy innovation and related funding opportunities, often short term. The notion of 'joined-up working' is central to the Scottish Executive's model of developing social inclusion and improving social justice. This study provides some signposts as to how this may be conceptualised and how it might be better achieved.

3. Context

This chapter provides the context for the more detailed findings of the study. We first describe the three local authorities and discuss the strategic level of collaboration in each. We then provide a brief account of the six schools and a description of the sample of five young people from each, focusing on current issues for them both in and out of school.

The three local authorities

Douglasshire Council in the west of Scotland is an area of mixed urban, rural and isolated communities, many relying historically on coal mining. With declining traditional industries, Douglasshire suffers the highest rate of unemployment of the three; indeed it has the highest rate of any local authority in Scotland. (See Table 3.1)

Table 3.1 Unemployment rates (%), claimant count (8 February 2001)

	Men	Women	Total
Douglasshire	14.4	6.0	10.7
Wallace City	3.9	1.1	2.5
Glenmore	4.6	1.7	3.2
Scotland	7.1	2.4	4.9

Source: *Labour Market Statistics March 2001: Scotland, National Statistics*

Wallace City is a large urban authority in the east of Scotland, with a thriving economy and the lowest unemployment rate of the three; well below the national average. However, there are significant areas of multiple deprivation, reflected in the high proportion of children entitled to free school meals; above the national average and the highest in the three local authorities. (See Table 3.2)

Table 3.2 Free school meal entitlement

	All sectors		Secondary	
	Number of pupils on register	% recorded as entitled to free meals	Number of pupils on register	% recorded as entitled to free meals
Douglasshire	18,841	21.9	7,743	18.4
Wallace City	49,071	22.9	18,654	17.7
Glenmore	15,473	8.6	6,465	6.3
Scotland	745,268	20.3	306,159	17.2

Source: *School Meals in Education Authority Schools 1999-2000*, Scottish Executive

Glenmore Council is a large rural authority in the south of Scotland with a low population density and few large towns. While the unemployment rate is below the Scottish average, Glenmore's economic situation has been deteriorating because of reliance on a narrow range of industries and the impact of structural changes on sectors such as agriculture. Average gross weekly earnings of full-time employees are below the rural Scotland average. It has a very low uptake of free school meals which, it has been suggested, is partly due to the stigma attached.

Education

There are some important differences related to education across the three local authorities, not least in the levels of exclusion from school with Douglasshire having the highest rates of exclusion and Glenmore Council the lowest.

In terms of attainment of school pupils in Douglasshire and Wallace City are very close to the national average of 75 per cent of S4 roll with 5+ Standard Grades at 1–4. Glenmore had higher educational attainment with 80 per cent. Wallace City had the highest figures for unauthorised absence, with 13 half days per pupil compared to three half days in Douglasshire and two half days in Glenmore (national average is five half days per pupil). (*Attendance and Absence in Scottish Schools 1999/2000*, Scottish Executive.)

Social work

In Glenmore Council and Wallace City, social work services are delivered by a separate department but social work and education in Douglasshire merged into a single department during the course of the research. Wallace City has a higher than average proportion of services provided by private and voluntary agencies and, as will be seen, this is reflected in the range of services accessed in relation to pupils at risk of exclusion. In contrast, Douglasshire inherited few services within its geographical boundaries at local government reorganisation and has had to establish a range of services. In Glenmore Council access to services is affected by distance and limited public transport.

There was a major issue of staff recruitment and retention amongst social workers in children and family teams and the pressures of statutory work in child protection meant that involvement in inter-agency working with children at risk of school exclusion could be problematic. Glenmore Council has the lowest proportion of children looked after of the three local authorities: 7 per 1,000. This compares to 9 per 1,000 in Douglasshire and 12 per 1,000 in Wallace City and the national average of 10 per 1,000 (Scottish Executive, 2001b).

Inter-agency working in the three local authorities

Douglasshire

The Youth Strategy is a multi-disciplinary initiative involving close cooperation between education staff, social work staff, educational psychologists, voluntary agencies and other professionals. There is a hierarchical, multi-disciplinary decision-making structure, with two levels of School Based Inter-agency Meetings. Both are case based, local authority policy stating that decisions should not be made at these meetings unless pupils and parents are present. Both meetings discuss pupils who have a wide range of difficulties including learning difficulties, social and behavioural problems, medical and/or physical difficulties.

The 'first level' School-Based Inter-agency Meeting is designed to provide the school with a 'straightforward mechanism for planning the needs of children and young people from within the range of resources that the school has access to directly – both within the school and via the normal contracted relationships with visiting professionals' (Douglasshire Council policy document).

First level meetings are held monthly in the school, convened/chaired by a member of the school's senior management team. The aims are to plan for the educational needs of a young person and, if appropriate, to plan re-integration after a period of temporary exclusion.

Referrals to this level of meeting were mainly to do with behaviour in class and are made exclusively by school staff. Pupils referred were already receiving some in-school support such as being given a behaviour monitoring sheet (conduct card), receiving learning support or having their attendance regularly checked. If a social worker was involved with a young person they would also be expected to attend.

Local authority policy documents state that when it can be shown that resources and approaches available to first level meetings have been 'reasonably exhausted', then a 'second level' of inter-agency meeting will be convened by a member of the social work department. These meetings are the forum that manages access to all the wider authority resources. Possible outcomes from this meeting could include planned accommodation of young people or access to special education provision within or outwith the authority. Meetings are held monthly on predetermined dates in the school. All such meetings throughout the local authority are managed and chaired by one officer from the social work department.

At local authority level, there is an inter-agency prioritisation group, consisting of senior officers from educational psychology, social work and education who make decisions about resources and budgets.

Wallace City

Wallace City recently revised its policy for working together to provide integrated support for vulnerable children. School Based Inter-agency Meetings are a key focus of this strategy. Guidelines were produced to clarify and regularise these meetings which aim to:

> **promote social inclusion** and to **raise educational standards** by planning appropriate curricular and care strategies to support the child in full participation, to remain with their family in their local school and in their local community. Its ability to do so flows from the more comprehensive view of the children's needs which a multi-agency perspective offers. *(Wallace City policy document, emphasis in original)*

The broad referral criteria apply to young people at risk of exclusion; looked after; assessed as having complex learning needs; at risk of offending or of serious substance abuse; 'in need' (for example those who may be isolated, depressed, with mental health problems, etc.). Referrals come from the school and other participating agencies such as social work.

Although the policy document states that any one of the core membership may chair the group, in the two schools studied the meetings were chaired by a member of the school's senior management team, who was also responsible for the administration of the meetings.

A series of different inter-agency meetings beyond the school form a structure both for further assessment and for decision making about wider resources, for example out of local authority placement. Such meetings would be called if the School Based Inter-agency Meeting felt they had exhausted support in the school and the neighbourhood.

Glenmore Council

School Based Inter-Agency Meetings have a narrower remit than those in the other two local authorities. They form part of a staged procedure in relation to the education of pupils who require support for learning. They are:

> the appropriate forum for managing the school's involvement in the staged procedures for joint planning for the education and care of children and young people with serious social emotional and behavioural difficulties … this structure will bring together those people with responsibility and expertise to support the school community as a whole. (*Glenmore Council policy document, 1997*)

The principal aims of the meetings are to coordinate the development of individual programmes for such pupils, which promote self-esteem, social skills and an increased sense of responsibility and to contribute to whole-school strategies for promoting positive behaviour and good attendance.

The meetings are usually chaired by a member of the school senior management team to assess, coordinate assessment, recommend appropriate strategies, and identify appropriate resources for those young people referred. A key role within this is 'to ensure that parents or carers are informed of a referral to the [inter-agency meeting] and are actively and positively involved in the subsequent programmes' (Glenmore Council policy paper).

In 1997, Glenmore Council established a joint social work and education resource for children with social, emotional and behavioural difficulties. It provides linkwork support to schools through individual work, in-class support or groupwork; day provision for pupils unable to remain in mainstream education; and outreach support through individual work or groupwork.

Following the setting up of this joint provision, a local authority-wide liaison group was established involving education, social work, educational psychology, and child psychiatry to make decisions on additional resources in individual cases and to provide a strategic overview of needs and resources.

The six schools

All schools in our study were publicly funded local authority managed comprehensive secondary schools. In Scotland there are no 'opted out' schools or state funded selective schools. There is a level of devolved school management, but head teachers may be seen to have less autonomy, and local authorities to have more power to require and monitor policy implementation, than in England. Two of the schools are Catholic which draw from a wide catchment area, and some of the other school populations may have been significantly affected by parental choice. As the three local authorities varied widely, so did the six schools.

Mooredge Academy (Douglasshire) is the largest of the six schools, a non-denominational secondary school in a small industrial town with a population of just under 10,000. The handbook stresses partnership between parents and teachers in developing good discipline. The discipline policy sets out the following procedures in dealing with discipline: verbal warning by teacher; discipline log; punishment exercise; referral to principal teacher; temporary isolation in another class; departmental behavioural timetable; referral to senior management team who may invoke change of timetable/class, detention, behavioural timetables, joint working with external agencies, referral to the School Based Inter-agency Meetings; exclusion.

St Mary's (Douglasshire) is a Catholic secondary school which, following a merger in 1998, now serves the entire local authority area both rural and urban. This school has two campuses, with S5 and S6 in one campus only. The handbook sets out a consistent approach to dealing with indiscipline including: verbal warning; punishment exercises; internal detention; removal from class; departmental conduct card; referral to assistant head teacher who may take action including detention; weekly conduct card; exclusion from subject; recommendation to head teacher for exclusion.

Braehead (Wallace City), the smallest school, is a non-denominational secondary school serving a catchment area of multiple deprivation. Over half of the pupils are entitled to free school meals. The handbook says that if students disrupt classroom work they are disciplined and if necessary removed from the classroom. There is an in-school support base. For serious breaches of discipline, students can be excluded. Since the mid 1970s this school has been involved in innovative inter-agency practice with young people in difficulty. They may refer pupils to a recently established link project staffed by the social work and education departments.

St John's (Wallace City) is a Catholic inner-city school with a strong tradition of educational attainment and a wide catchment area. This school is presently located on two campuses awaiting a new school being built. S1–S3 are on one campus and

S4 on another close by. The school handbook states that the approach to discipline is based on respect for other people. This school has recently set up a multi-agency learning base that aims to assist pupils to return to mainstream classes and to support those with behavioural/education difficulties.

Lochside Academy (Glenmore) is a large non-denominational secondary school serving a small town of some 13,700 people and surrounding villages. It has a history of supporting initiatives that encourage positive behaviour. The handbook states that the behavioural policy aims to recognise, reward and reinforce good work, good behaviour and good attendance through positive rewards which include: praise by staff, certificate of commendation (for non-curricular achievement); certificate of academic endeavour (for high levels of effort in class); certificate of academic achievement (for high grades in subject examinations); and merit certificates (for behavioural improvement). Sanctions include: punishment exercises; instruction to move seat; a behaviour card; detention; referral to school management; removal from the teaching group (which may involve movement to another teaching group or placement in a behavioural support group); exclusion.

Benview (Glenmore) is a small non-denominational secondary school serving a small town of just under 6,000 people and surrounding villages. It promotes positive behaviour in three main ways: praise by staff; positive referral slips (a sheet congratulating the pupil on their success); merit awards and merit certificates. The school handbook sets out the following ways of dealing with negative behaviour: told to behave; moved to work elsewhere; punishment exercise; detention; sent 'on-call' (moved to work on own with another teacher); exclusion.

Comparing the six schools

There are significant differences across the schools with respect to academic attainment. In Benview, 88 per cent of the S4 roll gained 5+ Standard Grades at 1–4. St John's was next with 77 per cent and three schools clustered just below this: St Mary's (74 per cent); Mooredge (72 per cent) and Lochside (71 per cent). Braehead, however, fell well below with only 35 per cent of the S4 roll gaining these grades (*Examination results in Scottish Schools 1999*, Scottish Executive).

While acknowledging issues of using free school meal entitlement as a proxy for social deprivation, the figures do indicate the marked differences across the six schools. The school with the highest figures is Braehead in Wallace City with 50.7 per cent of pupils recorded as entitled to free school meals. Next comes Mooredge in Douglasshire with 24.8 per cent of pupils entitled. St Mary's in Douglasshire and St John's in Wallace City have 15.7 per cent and 13.3 per cent of pupils entitled respectively. The two schools in Glenmore have the lowest proportion of pupils entitled to free school meals: Lochside (7.2 per cent) and Benview (6.1 per cent)

There are considerable variations in the rates of exclusion across the six schools. Table 3.3 lists schools in order of the proportion of pupils receiving free school meals. It can be seen that for the most part the rate of exclusions from school follows the order of social deprivation as measured by uptake of free school meals. However, this does not explain the marked differences between, for example, St Mary's and St John's. Most research on disciplinary exclusion from school suggests that excluded pupils are not a homogeneous group but that a range of different factors are involved in the process which leads them to being excluded. Many of these factors are to do with aspects of school life and how schools use the process of exclusion. Effective inter-agency working is only one of a number of factors which affect rates of school exclusion. Professional ideologies, attitudes of staff and school ethos remain important factors in determining rates of school exclusion between similar schools.

Table 3.3 Exclusions from school 1999–2000

	Temporary	Removed from register	Total	Exclusions per 1000 pupils
Braehead	86	1	87	189
Mooredge	142	0	142	142
St Mary's	111	0	111	130
St John's	5	4	9	14
Lochside	33	0	33	34
Benview	26	0	26	46

The case study young people

Schools were asked to identify young people, male and female, who had been excluded or were at risk of exclusion, but whose case exemplified *how pupils can be supported effectively through inter-agency working*. The young people were in some respects very diverse, perhaps the only common feature being that one or more aspects of their lives were the subject of concern by professionals. We interviewed 22 male and 8 female young people aged between 12 and 15 years. Five were between 12 and 13, the rest were 14 or 15 years old.

National statistics, in both England and Scotland, suggest more than four-fifths of excludees are male. However the lack of attention paid to the experiences of young women in much other research led us to specify to schools that we wished our sample to be mixed. All pupils identified for the study were white. The small number of pupils from ethnic minorities in Scottish schools means that ethnicity does not figure as a key aspect of national statistics. We recognise that it may still of course be a significant aspect of exclusion at the level of some individual schools.

Table 3.4 summarises information gathered from young people directly, from their parents/carers and from professionals. The first part contains information about clearly collectable data, although this data in practice was often not gathered in one place. The records of busy professionals were often not up to date or organised in an easily accessible form. The second part of the Table reflects the accounts of various participants, and includes some labels which might sometimes be contested, by particular professionals. Nothing has however been included which was not raised in interviews with young people and their families, by, or with them.

Table 3.4 Overview of issues for the young people

Previously excluded	26
Record of Special Educational Needs	4
Referred to the Reporter	13
Attended the Children's Hearings	8
With foster carers	3
Non-recorded learning difficulties	9
Had been bullied	9
Mental health concerns	5
Diagnosed with 'medical' conditions with behavioural implications, e.g. ADHD	3
Current problems in family	17
Delinquency outwith school	17
Complex difficulties across a range of settings	14 (9 male and 5 female)

Most pupils excluded from school in Scotland, as in England, are excluded for a short time and return to their own school quickly and do not experience exclusion again. For many of these young people exclusion can therefore be seen as a reflection of their relationship with the disciplinary structures of the school, and no assumptions should be made about other difficulties in their lives. The criteria used in selecting young people for participation in this study meant that we did not include pupils who had been excluded from school but where no significant inter-agency work focus was regarded as necessary.

Analysis of the interviews with the young people, their parents and professionals, in addition to our observations of meetings, led to the development of a model of three clusters defined in terms of how wide-ranging and serious current issues in their lives were and the level of inter-agency support seen to be required. However we are not claiming that these three groupings (Table 3.5, 2, 3 and 4) reflect a typology of all excluded pupils. Such a model would have to include that much wider group of excluded pupils whose difficulties lie almost entirely in their relationships with school. This point is important as we do not wish to assert the necessity of inter-agency working for all pupils who are at risk of, or have experienced, disciplinary exclusion. Our study does not undermine the point made in other research that in terms of preventing exclusion the first and central point of action lies within the school (Parsons, 2000; Munn and others, 2001). This typology seems to be helpful in making sense of when, how and why inter-agency working was agreed. Typologies by their nature never map neatly onto real life but can help to make sense of it.

Table 3.5 Typology of excluded pupils

1. **School based problems – school solutions alone appropriate**

    School based difficulties. Excluded pupils really only discipline problem *for* the school (usually pupils who are temporarily excluded only once and for whom there are no other concerns). Individual discussion at School Based Inter-agency Meetings not usually necessary, although general staff development through discussion in the meetings may feed into alterations in aspects of disciplinary or pastoral practices.

2. **Problems mainly school based but some additional support required**

    Those who had presented challenging behaviour in school and who may have had some problems outside school in terms of their own mental health or difficulties in their family, but who, overall, were not seen to have a wide range of complex difficulties in their lives. Discussed at School Based Inter-agency Meetings once or occasionally and strategies agreed.

3. **Problems perceived to be associated with particular diagnosed special education needs for which additional support provided**

    Pupils with Records of Needs for difficulties other than simply implied in the term SEBD. Often young people with diagnosed conditions to which their behavioural difficulties may be considered to be related, e.g. Asperger's Syndrome or Attention Deficit Hyperactivity Disorder. Discussed fairly frequently at School Based Inter-agency Meetings, particularly when there are issues about challenging behaviour in school.

4. **Multiple problems identified across a range of settings requiring substantial additional support**

    Young people with complex difficulties across a range of settings. Pupils were included in this group if they were considered to have serious difficulties in school and their family situation and in the neighbourhood. Frequently on the agenda of School Based Inter-agency Meetings, strategies agreed, reviewed and revised.

Further detail of this analysis follows below and then forms the basis of the discussion of direct support and intervention in Chapter 5. It is important to acknowledge the subjectivity of the assessment of problems and difficulties in the lives of young people – often such problems are described through the eyes of different (usually professional) beholders. In this study, when we refer to the problems or difficulties in a young person's life, we mean those which were described or discussed *in interviews with young people* rather than just from a professional report.

Group 1:
School based problems – school solutions alone appropriate

No such pupils were included in the case studies. Re-integration strategies for those who had been excluded and who did not require any support beyond school were discussed in the School Based Inter-agency Meetings observed. Most excluded pupils, readmitted to the school, would not be discussed in any detail.

Group 2:
Problems mainly school based but some additional support required

There were 12 young people in this grouping, 10 male and two female. They were quite diverse in their experiences of school but tended not to be seen currently to have *major* issues outside school, either in their families or in the community. When they were temporarily excluded from school it was for the same range of reasons as the other pupils in the study, mainly general disruptiveness in class or for fighting in school. For some there were particular reasons, for example one pupil had been seen as highly disruptive when attending the same school as his sibling, but much less so when he moved schools. One young woman was friendless in school and had mental health problems, the other felt treated like a child at school. Both of these young women were in trouble over not wearing the school uniform. Some of the others were disengaged or having difficulties in accessing the curriculum. Others had no real history of trouble in school but had been involved in one major incident.

Bruce

Bruce is 15 years old. He does find some subjects difficult (he was receiving some learning support) and said there were a couple of teachers that he did not get on with. Things appeared to deteriorate quickly just before the summer holidays last year, culminating in his being excluded from school for fighting with another pupil. His mother was completely taken aback saying 'it was the last thing we ever expected from Bruce because he was getting on so well'.

Group 3:
Problems perceived to be associated with particular diagnosed special education needs for which additional support provided

Four young people in this study, one female and three male, had a Record of Special Educational Need, three of them as a result of what were perceived to be difficulties associated with a particular diagnosed medical condition. Two were diagnosed with ADHD (Attention Deficit Hyperactivity Disorder) and one as ADHD associated with Asperger's Syndrome. One further young man had a Record of Special Educational Need because of severe specific learning difficulties. (A further nine young people in the study were considered by their teachers to have general difficulties in accessing the school curriculum.) Predictably, for the first three Recorded pupils the schools identified issues associated with attention problems, impulsivity and 'behaviour dangerous in class'. Three of these young people had also been in trouble for retaliating and getting into fights when they were picked on by other pupils.

Rory
Rory is 13 years old and has a Record of Special Educational Need. When asked how he got on at school he answered 'not so bad, some of the time things go wuzzy'. When this happens he 'sits down' and is 'calmed' by the assistant head teacher. Rory is on medication for ADHD, has a speech difficulty and dyspraxia. The school described Rory's volatile and worsening behaviour in class and school, with sudden outbursts of temper when he would for example throw scissors across a classroom. Rory's mother said his behaviour at home was also deteriorating.

Group 4:
Multiple problems identified across a range of settings requiring substantial additional support

About half of the participants in this study were facing major difficulties in multiple aspects of their life, in their family, their community and at school. These young people were not drawn evenly from the case study schools but were in areas of economic disadvantage; five were in Braehead School, Wallace City Council, and three in Mooredge School, Douglasshire.

Some of these young people were dealing with very serious issues in their families, including violence and abuse, and parents with serious physical or mental health problems. Three were living with foster carers, and a fourth with relatives, for all or part of the time of our study. Several were considered to have a serious problem with their use of drugs, including alcohol, aerosols, and in one case heroin. All were involved in some level of delinquency outwith school.

This group of young people had all experienced temporary exclusion, in some cases for quite long periods; three had been excluded/removed from the register of previous schools. At the time of the interviews one was still temporarily excluded from a case study school. Several were temporarily excluded during the period of study. One of the 14 had no major problems of directly challenging behaviour in school but she truanted and had a serious range of other problems. The others were all described by their schools as presenting the range of the in-school problems often identified in other research as reasons for exclusion, mainly fighting between pupils and general disruptiveness. Descriptions included 'insolence to teachers', 'refusing to work', 'mucking about in class', 'always in trouble', 'walks out of class', 'vandalism in school', 'fighting and bullying'.

Lindsay

Lindsay is 13 years old and now enrolled in her third secondary school. Her mother says she was 'asked to take Lindsay out of her first secondary school'. Lindsay 'lasted less than a week' at her second school before coming to Braehead. Lindsay is described by the school as 'wild, completely uncivilised, and completely uneducable in school' (AHT). There are also concerns around gang fights and relationship in the neighbourhood. Her guidance teacher described her as 'not being able to step back from a fight'. Lindsay is thought to be beyond control of her mother with whom she fights.

All were considered to be dealing with difficulties relating to school and their families and their neighbourhood.

Conclusion

In this chapter we have described the very diverse local authorities and schools in which our study took place. We have discussed the contexts for inter-agency decision making and in particular the School Based Inter-agency Meetings, identifying key differences and similarities in their operation. We also provided an overview of the different groups of young people interviewed as part of this study.

4. School Based Inter-agency Meetings

When discussing inter-agency initiatives with both local authorities and schools it was clear that the focus for such work was seen to be the School Based Inter-agency Meeting. In each local authority they have a wider remit than just preventing or responding to exclusion. There are also important differences in relation to their focus on wider strategy or individual cases.

The meetings in each school reflect the level of involvement of particular professionals and access to particular types of support available. All the meetings reviewed and explored existing strategies as well as identifying and recommending new resources. Sometimes schools were looking for advice and/or information from professionals; for some of the pupils these were also seen as review meetings; and for others the meetings were part of a process or strategy which would result in their exclusion/removal from the register.

In this chapter we will discuss the School Based Inter-agency Meetings, identifying issues relating to participation, attendance, recommendations and resources.

Participation and attendance at meetings

The issue of meetings as strategic and/or case based is reflected in who attends. As Table 4.1 illustrates, all those attending the meetings in Douglasshire Council were directly involved with a particular young person and their family, and, importantly, would include the young person and their parents/guardian. Glenmore and Wallace City Councils have a wide ranging core membership and case specific professionals would be invited to join the meeting for the discussion of a particular young person. Parents and young people are usually not invited to meetings in Braehead, St John's or Lochside, whereas in Benview parents, although not pupils, may be present.

Table 4.1 Membership of School Based Inter-agency Meetings

	Douglasshire Council 'First level' meetings	Douglasshire Council 'Second level' meetings	Wallace City Council	Glenmore Council
School Senior Management	Chair (Mooredge School)	✔	Chair	Chair
Guidance staff	Chair (St Mary's School) + Case specific	Case specific	✔	✔
Learning Support	Case specific	Case specific	✔	✔
Social Work representative		Chair	✔	✔
Representative from the Council-wide Support Centre			✔	✔
Educational Welfare Officer			✔	
Voluntary agencies (e.g. local youth project		Case specific	✔	✔
Educational Psychologist	✔	✔	✔	✔
Community Education			✔	
School doctor/ nurse		Case specific	✔	✔
Community police representative			✔	
Other case specific person	Case social worker if already allocated	✔	✔	✔
Pupil	✔	✔		
Parent(s)/ Guardian(s)	✔	✔		Occasionally (in Benview school only)

In Douglasshire Council the attendance of parents and pupils at the meetings was seen as necessary for their participation in discussion and decisions which would affect them. 'Parents and pupils are seen as being right in the middle of the decision making process and if they're not there [the inter-agency meeting] certainly does not go ahead' (Senior School Manager). For both schools in this local authority pupil intake was from a large geographical area, and the economics and practicalities of parents attending the meetings did present some unresolved issues. For example, the assistant head teacher at Mooredge School recognised that many pupils attending the school lived in a housing estate some distance away. If parents were asked to attend a meeting this meant additional costs to the family (in time and money), though almost all parents/guardians did.

'We are talking a journey of five or six miles [to the school] .... It's £2.10 return on the bus, and if mum or dad are fortunate enough to have a job, they will certainly not give up a morning or afternoon's wages to come to a meeting.' *(Assistant head teacher)*

All those parents/guardians interviewed in Douglasshire had attended a School Based Inter-agency Meeting, and almost all had found them intimidating – at least initially. One young person from Mooredge School admitted 'I find it a bit scary' and his mother recalled that she had been so nervous about attending her first meeting that she asked *her* mother to go to the meeting with her. However, both parents and young people were unanimous in the view that their attendance at these meetings was important, with one young person remarking that they wanted to hear what was being said about them 'to their face'. If issues were ongoing and parents had attended several meetings, some of them said that they found it increasingly easier to participate and give their view. The minutes of meetings from both St Mary's and Mooredge did indicate that some parents and young people were actively involved in the discussions and their views recorded. Many parents had had a negative experience of school and found it difficult to feel at ease there, but the room in which the meeting was held could also hinder participation. For example, in Mooredge School the meetings were held in the corner of a large room of computers and although attempts were made to arrange the furniture in a more 'user-friendly' way it remained a room dominated by computers. In St Mary's School the meetings were given a level of formality by being held in the 'Board Room', which led this mother to remark:

'We go in and sit in the Board Room around that big table. I think it depends who you're sitting next to as to how intimidated you are [laughs].' *(Ian's mother)*

The participation of young people and their parents/guardians in the meetings could also be hindered by language that was not familiar to them. For example, at one meeting observed at Mooredge School, a young person clearly stated that he did not want his present situation to be changed and the comment was made 'so we will keep the status quo then', prompting the young person to screw up his face in puzzlement; but he did not ask for an explanation and his puzzlement was not picked up by others in the meeting.

The focus in most meetings was on solutions and support. Fears of punishment or retribution were usually dispelled quickly and the meetings were generally seen by parents, if not always the young people, as supportive. Some parents had, until this point, blamed themselves for not being able to cope with/solve the 'problem' and they welcomed the opportunity to discuss things. For some parents the meetings 'with all these people round the table' signified that things were now being taken 'seriously'; that the issue was no longer just between them and the school, and that things would change. However, these expectations did sometimes lead to some frustrations and disillusionment, as discussed later in this chapter.

In the other two local authorities young people and parents were not usually invited to attend the meetings although they were told that a meeting was taking place, asked for their opinion and told afterwards what decisions had been made. Benview School did occasionally invite parents. Pre- or post-School Based Inter-agency Meetings often took place in a smaller sub-group of involved professionals, or, more usually, with the guidance teacher or social worker. However, even for those young people who have been told about a meeting, it was sometimes difficult for them to recall what had happened, as the following comments illustrate:

'I cannae mind when, but I can remember being told that I was going to be talked about that my name was brought up.' *(Bruce, Lochside School, Glenmore Council)*

'I got told about one [meeting] but I don't really know [what happened] because I never know when they're doing it …' *(Maureen, St John's School, Wallace City Council)*

However some young people and parents were well informed about the meetings, with this mother feeling very involved in the decision making process:

'[The Assistant head teacher] phoned me about that [placement in off site unit] and we talked about it, and they asked me how I felt about [son] going there. [Assistant head teacher] didn't just go ahead and say "I have got a space there, I am going to shove him there out of the road" sort of thing … I was asked how I felt about it.' *(Colin's mother, Braehead School, Wallace City Council)*

The issue of young people and their parents participating in decision making is an important one. All three local authorities had policies which were aimed at involving young people and their parents in decision making – the difference between them being that Douglasshire chose to do it by direct participation, while Wallace City and Glenmore had strategies to inform and involve parents and young people outwith the meetings. But the issue is still debated, as indicated below:

'I think the policy about practice would indicated that parents and children should be involved at these meetings … but they are still professional meetings … it's a difficult balance … the distinction gets made where there are resource implications and there is a professional argument to be had before, that shouldn't be had in front of parent or child.' *(Senior Education Officer, Glenmore Council)*

Another issue related to the participation of young people and parents in these meetings is that of confidentiality. When young people and parents are present they are fully aware of the information shared at that meeting, and, in Douglasshire Council, that this information is shared only between those professionals who have a direct input into their situation. Many parents and young people (in all three local authorities) said that they felt uncomfortable about professionals discussing them, but those in Douglasshire Council usually also commented that this was necessary if things were to change/improve. For example, Kenneth (a pupil at Mooredge School) said that people at the meetings 'needed to know' if they were to be able to help. In Glenmore and Wallace City Councils there are policies relating to the confidentiality of information and how this should be shared with the family and between the professionals at the meeting, but the strategic remit and wide ranging membership of the meetings would appear to mitigate against the young people and their parents having any direct control over what information may be disclosed and to whom. For example, a member of a Braehead School meeting made the following comment:

'I wonder if pupils attending [inter-agency meetings] would modify what was being said?' *(Voluntary agency representative, Wallace City Council)*

The participation of young people and parents attending these meetings therefore depends on whether the meetings are purely case based or combine discussions of particular pupils along with a wider strategic remit. Those meetings with a strategic remit had an overall responsibility for planning support services for vulnerable young people within the school and relating these to neighbourhood provision. The remit of the meetings directly affect which professionals attend, the type of discussion that takes place, and the kind of decisions and strategies that are recommended. Figure 4.1 locates the School Based Inter-agency Meetings in relation to:

- whether their purpose included strategic planning of service delivery as well as case discussion;
- whether pupils and parents participate in the meeting.

This model will be developed later to include the advantages and disadvantages of each type of meeting.

Figure 4.1 Initial matrix: participation and nature of School Based Inter-agency Meetings

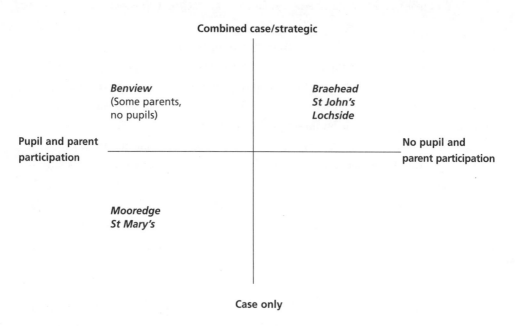

The meetings were prioritised by most participating agencies, but regular attendance of some key personnel was an issue in all three local authorities. In Douglasshire Council the educational psychologist should attend both meetings at both levels. In St Mary's School this did regularly happen, but in Mooredge the educational psychologist was on long-term sick leave and there was no replacement. This led to both school staff and parents becoming angry and frustrated at delayed assessments and delayed action that hinged on the intervention of a psychologist. The frequency of the meetings was also a problem for some core members in Glenmore Council. These meetings had been held monthly, and now take place fortnightly. The increase in frequency meant that some professionals were not able to attend every meeting and a compromise was reached whereby some agencies would continue to attend monthly. This agreement was very recent and the effect (if any) upon decisions made at the meetings could not be assessed.

For some professionals the time taken to attend School Based Inter-agency Meetings had to be 'found' among many other pressing commitments. For example, at St Mary's School (Douglasshire Council) a GP had attended several meetings, but commented that although she felt it important to attend the meetings and support parents and young people, it was 'not in her job description'. Parents in Douglasshire Council were very aware of who attended the meetings and who didn't, because these were people who had a very direct role in the services and support they received. The attendance of social workers – as case workers and as representatives – was an issue in all three local authorities. The non-attendance of social work representation has particular implications for inter-agency work as often the schools depend on a social work link to liaise directly with the family and their perspective is valued by schools as important for a holistic assessment. In Douglasshire Council there had been a representative of the social work youth team attending the first level meetings, but, immediately prior to this research, this had stopped because staff were no longer available for this. In Lochside School there had been social work representation at only two of the previous eight meetings (September–December 2000), which led this official to acknowledge:

> 'There was a knock-on from a recruitment crisis – that made it difficult for schools to have someone consistent in terms of School Based Inter-agency Meetings and that is an issue.' *(Social Work Senior Manager, Glenmore Council)*

Discussion and recommendations made at the meetings

The remit of the meetings as combined case/strategic or only case based influences all aspects of the meeting – not only who should attend, but the discussions, the information shared and the recommendations made. As discussed in Chapter 3 these meetings were not exclusively about pupils at risk of exclusion, or as a way of accessing out of school resources, so discussions in all the schools and in all the meetings were varied and wide ranging, though the overall format was similar. For example, the person who had referred the young person to the meetings was asked to give their reasons for this. Others in the meeting with any direct knowledge of the young person, or their circumstances, were then asked to contribute. In those meetings with a combined case/strategic remit some core members would participate in a consultative capacity, whilst others would be able to offer direct support and resources.

The discussion and resulting decisions could then take various forms from, for example, the identification of a short-term intervention by one other agency, to several interventions happening simultaneously, as illustrated by Figure 4.2.

Figure 4.2 Diagram of School Based Inter-agency Meetings

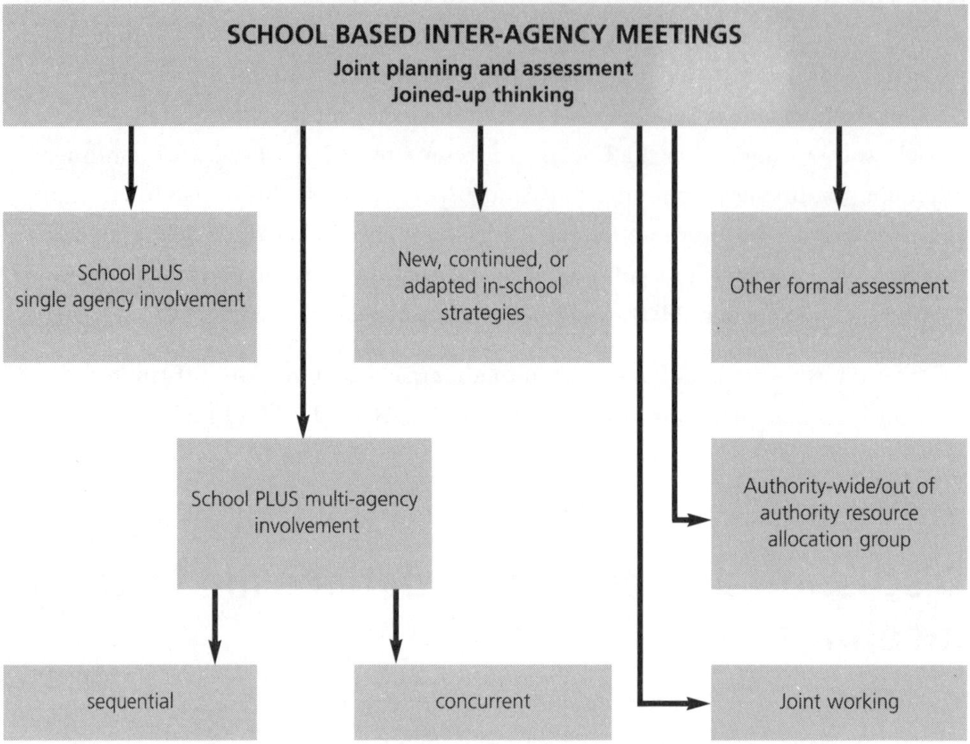

School Based Inter-agency Meetings were not always about new plans and strategies, or accessing resources. For example, the meetings themselves sometimes functioned as direct work with pupils, especially in Douglasshire Council, but also sometimes in the other two local authorities. At the first level meetings in Douglasshire Council the purpose of the meeting was sometimes to talk through the issues or problems identified for the young person and to review progress. At one first level meeting observed at Mooredge School there was a review of the various in school strategies that had been put in place for a young person. These included an attendance card and a behaviour card and daily contact with their guidance teacher. At this meeting there was a general consensus that things had improved and the young person was asked if they felt ready to 'come off' the cards. The young person and their parent were delighted with the suggestion and agreed. It was also agreed that there would be no need for another review meeting. The young person had attended a total of three first level meetings over the previous school term. It seems that for some young people and their parents that the process of that discussion *in itself* may be supportive. Schools in Glenmore and Wallace City Councils offered this support in smaller, case-based multi-professional meetings prior to the formal inter-agency meetings.

The two meetings observed at St John's (Wallace City Council) were the most strategic and focused of all the participating schools, though this could be because of the particular time of the school year in which they were held. For example, one meeting discussed the intake for the next school year – highlighting those who had identified needs or where there may be cause for concern – and discussing the strategies which needed to be put in place for these pupils. The other meeting focused on the transition of third year pupils to the senior annexe – with an emphasis on making provision for continuing support and putting in place any additional resources thought necessary. Another aspect of these meetings was the planning of *joint working* – with the school and a local voluntary agency making plans to run a group together in the school. As explained by the voluntary agency representative:

> 'Around summertime we review all our work for the coming year … and we encourage school to, if you like, make bids in terms of what they want from us in relation to group work, … so we are an integral part of the [school based inter-agency] meetings … the others in the [meetings] use us, and use us appropriately.' *(Voluntary agency representative, St John's School)*

At these meetings those present would be asked to be pro-active and 'put forward' names of pupils who may benefit from groupwork. There would be ongoing feedback to the meeting for the duration of the group and an evaluation report when it ended.

The meetings in Glenmore and Wallace City Councils had a regular core membership, and were often able to have frank and open discussions. In both these local authorities the histories of the agencies represented in the meetings, and those of the schools, were often well established. The individuals concerned were also often well known to each other and this could result in an informed and focused discussion:

> 'Where we've got a strong relationship with the school it's really quite simple – it's about them having a fairly clear idea of what might be on offer, and how we might respond … and so it makes it quite simple.' *(Voluntary Project representative)*

Although meetings with a core membership were able, over time, to develop a particular rapport between those professionals who regularly attend, in all three local authorities School Based Inter-agency Meetings had a considerable staff development impact. Across all professionals there was a recognition that such a forum led to a better understanding of what other professionals could do and the restraints under which they operated. Particularly in the school setting, guidance, learning support and behaviour support teachers were able to see links and synthesise their approaches and strategies with those of other professionals. Through the meetings there was an increased knowledge of the practical support that could be offered by each agency. As mentioned by parents, the involvement of other agencies was seen as an indication of shared responsibility and concerns.

> 'I find it quite amazing, you're sitting at these meetings and someone will say something "where did that come from?" and you're thinking, well, that kind of explains what happened that week then … the inter-agency meetings that I've attended, everyone has put in their information and from that there is usually pretty productive discussions as to where to go next.' *(Guidance teacher)*

Poverty and deprivation in the area of Braehead School in Wallace City Council meant that a wide range of resources seemed available to support the many vulnerable young people who attended the school. The meetings in this school had the largest and most diverse core membership which also involved community police, and community education workers who run a youth club based in the school and in other centres. Those attending the meeting were therefore able to comment on many aspects of what was happening in the community which may affect relationships in and out of school. The minutes of one meeting in Braehead (which discussed eight referrals) recorded 22 different agencies which were considered as 'possible resources' for supporting those referred. These ranged from a joint funded education and social work unit which offered part-time education and a national helpline for those suffering from insomnia, to the many small voluntary agencies which offered specific support for those who were self harming, taking drugs, or who may have been bereaved. The tone of the meetings observed was of the school 'not giving up' and continually adapting its own resources to work in conjunction with others to support young people in all areas of their lives.

Most of the time spent in the combined strategic/case based meetings was allocated to discussing particular young people. In both Wallace City and Glenmore the strategic remit of the meeting was evident while discussing individual referrals but was also used for planning purposes. An advantage of the core membership in these local authorities was the ability of some representatives to offer 'on the spot' support by, for example, agreeing to make a home visit. In Lochside School (Glenmore Council) the representative of the local youth project was able to inform the meeting that it would be possible for a young person to join a particular group in the project, and in Braehead School the representative from the support unit attached to the school could also tell the meeting if there were vacancies in the project. This knowledge of availability, and ability to immediately access resources, not only saved time, but directly involved those participating in the meeting in activating decisions made. Schools may also discuss the identification of pupils and possible mentors for a mentoring programme; the distribution of an information sheet for school staff informing them about the inter-agency meetings; the approach to be made to the social work department about lack of representation at meetings; and proactive planning for joint work. The case-specific remit of meetings in Douglasshire Council did not facilitate discussions of this nature.

The status and profession of those chairing the meetings varied (see Table 4.1) and did appear to have an effect on some discussions and decisions made. For example, Braehead School was the only school where the head teacher regularly chaired the meetings. Although this did give a clear message as to the priority given to these meetings it also appeared to give priority to the school's view, and some professionals felt sidelined. Although the following statement does refer to this issue in the past tense, there was evidence to suggest that this is still an issue:

> 'I am frustrated with the practice that has been in [inter-agency] meetings, in particular the culture of them being school led.' *(Voluntary Project representative, Wallace City Council)*

The only local authority that had a social work representative chairing the meetings was Douglasshire. Interestingly this produced conflicting responses. In interviews with school staff and professionals it was generally felt that having a social work chair gave the meetings an added status and priority which they considered was necessary and important. However, in both St Mary's and Mooredge there appeared to be some tension regarding the remit of the second level meeting which was largely perceived to be as a result of having a social work chairperson. As already mentioned, the first level meeting was the forum for discussing further in-school support – together with input from the educational psychologist. There was, however, an understanding by school staff that they would have exhausted all supports available to them prior to referring to a second level meeting:

> 'At [the second stage of meetings] it's a different set of circumstances for everybody concerned because the chair is from social services and what we're saying as a school is that we have absolutely exhausted all of the supports that we can put in place and we're now looking for some kind of support from the community to take it forward.' *(Senior School Manager)*

In one second level meeting observed at St Mary's School a pupil was referred because the school felt strongly that they had done everything they could to support him. The increasingly dangerous behaviour of the pupil led the school to recommend that the pupil should now be moved to a special school. The social work chair and the mother both disagreed with this view and an attempt was made to get the school to agree to continuing their support with revised strategies and plans, but this was unsuccessful. The atmosphere in the meeting was tense and although a decision was made to apply for a place in a special school, the underlying issue of the school coming to the meeting with the explicit aim of accessing out of school resources was not resolved. Some school staff felt their professional judgement, that the school could 'no longer fully meet the identified needs' of the pupil referred, was being questioned. However the social work chair of the second level meetings was quite clear that the remit was to discuss and plan for both in-school and out of school strategies. The case based nature of the meetings meant that there was no opportunity for those present to resolve the issue because the next case based meeting – involving several different people – was due to begin.

The level of demands on agencies and schools highlighted issues of professional boundaries and difficulties in inter-agency working. Although the value of providing a holistic plan for a young person was shared by all those we interviewed there were nonetheless tensions and issues at the structural, practical and personal levels. These were often identified when assessing a young person's needs.

> 'in spite of all the informal relationships … I think we get into real difficulties about assessing a child's needs – we still retreat behind professional lines and say "it's a social work problem", or "it's an education problem" … ' (*Coordinator, Joint funded initiative, Wallace City Council*)

Increased workloads and changes in policy and practice appeared to add, sometimes, to myths and stereotypes of 'other' professionals, in particular the view held by many school staff that social workers should play a key role in day to day home–school liaison. An education officer made the following comment:

'I have a social work background – and what I feel is there is a very clear miscomprehension between the different agencies about what social work is about and the benchmark whereby social work becomes involved … quite frequently I will hear staff talking about the need for a social worker to be allocated to a particular case, and I will know from my experience they are not even close to what would warrant a social worker … ' (*Education Officer, Glenmore Council*)

Communication both at and between inter-agency meetings was also difficult, with few documents being exchanged. Making contact by phone was often described as a matter of 'luck'. This was also reflected in professional record keeping where involvement of other agencies was rarely mentioned. Important information, such as dates of a Children's Hearing were not always shared.

Conclusion

What unites all those involved in the School Based Inter-agency Meetings is their participation in joint and joined-up assessment, discussion and decision making to support vulnerable young people. Almost all the professionals interviewed spoke of the importance of the meetings for sharing information, hearing other perspectives, 'putting faces to names', clearing up misunderstandings, and learning more about what other professionals do. There was a general feeling by those who attended the meetings that they were about developing whatever strategies were necessary to support vulnerable young people in their schools and in their neighbourhoods.

The issue of whether or not young people and parents should attend meetings is of current concern, and various advantages and disadvantages of both approaches were observed. The challenge for inter-agency meetings is to ensure full and informed participation in decisions which may, or may not, be best served by young people and their parents attending such a forum. Matters of confidentiality are clearly a major issue here.

Significant points arising from observation of School Based Inter-agency Meetings are listed below and Figure 4.3 summarises the pros and cons of different models of Meetings.

- **The meetings varied significantly in terms of the focus of the meetings and in terms of the participation of young people, parents and professional staff.** Variations in attendance partly reflected whether the meetings were case based or combined case/strategic meetings.

- **Irregular attendance of some professionals was an issue in all three local authorities.** Staff from mental health agencies and very pressured social workers often did not attend.

- **In this study case based meetings increased involvement by young people and parents/carers but combined case/strategic meetings discussed and planned wider service delivery in relation to vulnerable young people and young people with SEBD.** There were issues of confidentiality when young people were discussed in case/strategic meetings when professionals not directly involved were present. However, such professionals were observed to make helpful suggestions.

- **There was limited evidence of systematic evaluation of the outcomes of the meetings, other than through the review of individual cases.**

- **All professional staff interviewed felt that the School Based Inter-agency Meetings were central to their work and felt that the *joint* working in the meetings did promote a *joined-up* view of pupils' lives.** A number of staff criticised limitations on resources. Some school staff felt that the problems were sometimes pushed back onto the school, whereas some other professionals felt that they were expected to solve the problems of the school.

- **Although it was clear that the School Based Inter-agency Meetings had increased awareness of the roles and responsibilities of other professionals, sometimes under pressure old loyalties and differences of professionals' judgement were still barriers to effective work.**

School Based Inter-agency Meetings in all three local authorities were the locus for inter-agency joined-up thinking which may, or may not, result in further direct inter-agency collaboration. The success and effectiveness of these meetings relies on support, innovative thinking and not giving up – as will be evidenced in the following chapter when the direct work with the young people is discussed.

Figure 4.3 Pros and cons of different models of School Based Inter-agency Meetings

Combined case/strategic meetings
Without participation of young people and parents

- Possible 'on the spot' decisions/information about resources.
- Proactive planning.
- Meeting responsive to community needs.
- Can be supportive to staff. Promoted staff awareness of other professionals' roles and responsibilities.
- Helps diminish professional boundaries.
- Can be more informal.
- Encourages frank and open discussion.
- Promoted a wider approach to problem solving.
- Confidentiality issues regarding range of professionals at the meetings.
- Young person/families not present for discussions.
- Young people/families may not understand or agree with outcomes.
- Young people/families may not know who was present.

Combined case/strategic meetings
With participation of young people and parents

- Possible 'on the spot' decisions/information about resources.
- Proactive planning.
- Meeting responsive to community needs.
- Case element of the meeting more formal.
- Confidentiality issues were more transparent.
- Young people/families could disagree with decisions made.
- Promoted a wider approach to problem solving.
- Young people/families have no control over who attends.
- Possible embarrassment when personal and family matters shared with professionals not directly involved with them.
- Large number of professionals made attending more intimidating.

Case based meetings with participation of young people/families

- Smaller group of staff directly involved with young people/families.
- Young people/families could engage directly with decisions.
- Confidentiality transparent.
- Less opportunity for professionals to develop ongoing relationships.
- Professionals less aware of other's roles and responsibilities.
- Meetings more formal.
- Professionals may not always express honest opinions.

5. The case studies

In Chapter 4 we discussed the School Based Inter-agency Meetings which are clearly central to the planning and review of direct work with young people. In this chapter we explore the strategies, decided by the meetings, for work with the young people in this study and look at how effective they were in preventing exclusion and in providing support. The meetings were, of course, not simply about preventing exclusion – they were also about providing support and help to vulnerable young people. The young people in this study were all identified by their schools as examples of how the school staff worked well together with other agencies in preventing or reducing exclusion. They were clearly not all picked because their school believed things to be resolved. Several of the young people were still facing significant difficulties and their schools were still having considerable trouble with them. So some of the work can be seen more realistically as being about *addressing* but not necessarily *solving* problems.

Sometimes the plans agreed in the meetings involved the work of a single agency, sometimes they involved a complex package of support involving several. For some young people one specific intervention seemed to be enough to help them to resolve some issues, or to provide enough support for them to sustain their position in school. For others, particularly those in the group with more complex difficulties, a range of different options had often been tried, sometimes as part of a package of support, sometimes, sequentially as one seemed unsuccessful, another idea would be tried.

This chapter addresses the broad issue of what seemed to count as effective in this work. There are, as we argued earlier, problematic aspects in this kind of discussion. It is clear that there are no absolute ways of establishing, in the real world, what is the precise effect of a specific intervention. Equally the methods used to assess outcomes can vary between the apparently objective and the subjective. In this chapter we look at the more objective outcomes of exclusion reduction and continued participation in mainstream school along with the more subjective perceptions of the professionals, the young people and their families.

Inter-agency work in supporting the case study pupils

Table 5.1 provides details of professionals interviewed. Others, who were not interviewed because of illness, availability, difficulties of access or failure to reply to our letters/phone calls included a classroom auxiliary, two psychiatrists, a community worker, the fire brigade and a community policeman.

Table 5.1 The range of professionals interviewed regarding case study pupils

Interviewees directly involved with pupils in the study	Number: 77
Social work staff	
Children and Families team	7
Specialist intensive work with young people	6
Education Welfare Officers	2
Educational Psychologists	6
School staff	
School managers	6
Guidance teachers	19
Learning Support	6
Behaviour Support	3
Off site education support	4
Voluntary projects	9
Child Protection Agency	1
Other	
Careers Service	1
Joint education/social work projects	4
	1
Health staff	1
Army	1

The range of support discussed below contains those mentioned as specific interventions or supports in interviews, by the young person and their parent/carer. We discuss the support provided in terms of the four groups identified earlier in terms of degree of difficulties and level of inter-agency focus (see Table 3.5).

Group 1:
School based problems – school solutions alone appropriate

We did not include any such pupils in our case studies, other research substantiating the view that for such pupils effective responses to exclusion lie in the school, its ethos, and approaches to discipline and pastoral care (Munn and others, 2000; Parsons, 2000). However, our observations and analysis of the inter-agency meetings, as suggested earlier, show that such pupils were regularly on the agenda of School Based Inter-agency Meetings as a consequence of their exclusion. Often if readmitted to school they were simply noted but sometimes there would be discussion of how successful particular school strategies had been and suggestions made about amending these.

Group 2:
Problems mainly school based but some additional support required (12 pupils)

These young people had been discussed at School Based Inter-agency Meetings once or occasionally but were not a regular feature on the agenda. The individual support strategies planned at the meetings and provided for these young people were often not different from the support provided for the young people with more complex difficulties, however they were more likely to have been a one-off intervention and more often regarded as successful. The additional support was mainly from a single agency beyond the school in addition to extra support being provided in school, for example from learning support, guidance or behaviour support teachers.

> 'They [Careers] help with my career choice and I do a lot of charity work and that with them – it goes down on my achievement and gives me a better chance, 'cause I'm quite sociable and that and can talk to people.' *(Andy)*

Figure 5.1 Support strategies (Group 2)

- Additional learning support.
- Behaviour support teacher.
- Extra support from guidance teacher.
- Reduced/modified timetable.
- Reduced timetable plus out of school placements.
- Small groupwork in school, jointly run by teacher and local specialist youth project.

(continued)

- Careers group in school.
- Involvement in community based specialist youth provision.
- Extra support from educational psychologist.
- Mediation.
- Change of school.
- Interview/work placement with Army.
- Support from Educational Welfare Officer (School Attendance Officer).
- Befriending scheme.

What was effective?

Ten of the 12 young people in this group were still attending school, mainly following a regular timetable and not being further excluded. One young man is part-time attending an education support project and one young woman is having difficulties attending school. The support provided here indicated that for some young people the provision of the *right support* at the *right time* in their lives may work. This does not necessarily suggest that all their school or other problems have been resolved but that either they feel that 'something has been done' or perhaps that they have been listened to. They may feel more confident that they can, through alterations to their timetable, avoid a particular class or subject where they tended to get into trouble. In two cases the young people, through involvement in careers focused support, were perhaps clearer about the possibilities beyond school and were able to decide to grit their teeth and stick it out. It is also clear that the schools had continued to provide in-school support, beyond the universal services, along with that decided by the School Based Inter-agency Meetings.

Bruce

Bruce's guidance teacher felt that 'the carpet had been swept from under his feet' and it was suggested that Bruce become involved in a group run, in the school, by the careers service. Bruce was already a member of the army cadets and had recently been on an army residential which had made him determined to join the army when he left school. This was encouraged and supported by the careers group who asked the army careers service to come and talk to them. Bruce enjoyed being in this group saying 'you do activities to help you think about what's going to happen when you leave school'. Bruce has since been 'doing fine' at school.

What was the inter-agency dimension to the support?

There were two aspects here, first the inter-agency dimension offered by School Based Inter-agency Meetings, and secondly through the agreed additional support. That offered to this group of young people tended to involve a single agency beyond the school, for example the careers project. Two pupils were supported through joint work between a single agency and the school, groupwork undertaken by a Guidance teacher together with a member of staff from a neighbourhood youth centre. Support from an educational psychologist was mainly in providing consultancy services to schools, rather than in individual work with young people, but this did happen occasionally. Some valued support was also provided by individuals with no formal qualifications, such as befrienders and sessional workers.

Group 3:

Problems perceived to be associated with particular diagnosed special education needs for which additional support provided (4 pupils)

There were four pupils with Records of Needs, three for specifically diagnosed, apparently medical conditions to which their behavioural difficulties tended to be attributed, and one for specific learning difficulties. These pupils were discussed fairly frequently at School Based Inter-agency Meetings, particularly when there are issues about challenging behaviour in school. These pupils had a very mixed experience of school.

Rory

The discussion at an earlier meeting was about the possibility of Rory moving to another school where he could attend a learning support base. But Rory's mother was unhappy about that because he had previously been bullied by peers who attend that school. She felt that if Rory could have sustained one-to-one support in his current mainstream school he would be able to learn. The decision of the latest meeting, however, was to apply for a place for Rory in a special school which was, reluctantly, accepted by his mother.

What was effective?

Two of the four pupils were still in mainstream school, although one spent considerable time being supported out of class. One was mainly on an out of school package, although it included time in an FE college, and the fourth was in the process of being transferred to a local authority special school for pupils with significant learning difficulties. There were therefore real issues as to whether three of these pupils could be seen as effectively included in school. However the support strategies used had prevented further formal disciplinary exclusion.

Figure 5.2 Support strategies (Group 3)

- Additional learning support.
- Behaviour support teacher.
- Extra support from guidance teacher.
- Reduced/modified timetable.
- Transfer to special school.
- Groupwork project for girls.
- Intensive in-school support : extraction for behaviour and learning support.
- Psychiatric consultations and medication.
- Social work support.
- Package of FE + work experience + school.
- Classroom auxiliary.

What was the inter-agency dimension to the support?

Again there were two aspects here, first the inter-agency dimension offered by the School Based Inter-agency Meeting itself, and secondly through the agreed additional support. Also three of the pupils in this group had been seen by psychiatric services and medication had been prescribed. Although the school doctor or nurse sometimes attended the meetings there was little communication between the school and the mental health services. Only in Glenmore was the consultant child psychiatrist involved in the formal structures of communication; she was part of the regional level of inter-agency meetings. The three young people who had been prescribed medication were based in the other two local authorities where communication between the hospital mental health services and the other agencies seemed quite problematic. This was also reflected in our inability to interview all the relevant mental health personnel in our study. There were clearly issues here about the role of schools in giving out and monitoring the impact of medication.

Group 4:

Multiple problems identified across a range of settings requiring substantial additional support (14 pupils)

'We have pupils who you think well ... we have managed to be with them and they have not offended, or that their drug involvement has not increased considerably – that they are still here, but the way it was looking was that they were going down the plug hole ...' *(Head teacher)*

The 14 young people considered to have a wide a range of difficulties across their lives were clearly a challenge to those professionals involved with them. They were much more likely to have been involved with a range of support services beyond those available in school. They were more likely to have a social worker allocated as a result of a statutory order, particularly in Douglasshire. The pattern of involvement with other agencies was very varied, sometimes according to the young people's difficulties but also to resource availability.

Figure 5.3 Support strategies (Group 4)

- Additional learning support.
- Behaviour support teacher.
- Extra support from guidance teacher.
- Reduced/modified timetable.
- Individual interviews/meetings.
- Groupwork by school staff.
- Groupwork by youth social work staff.
- Joint groupwork school staff/voluntary or local authority youth support workers.
- Planned regular phone calls with parents.
- Individual meetings with educational psychologist.
- Part-time attendance at education support unit.
- Transfer to work preparation project.
- Social work (Children and Families teams).
- Specialist youth social work agencies.
- Meeting with fire brigade.
- Meeting with community police.
- Mentoring project.
- Referral to young people's psychiatric unit.

Whether and how the support provided by different agencies and professionals was valued varied according to a number of factors, some of these to do with the young person and their family and some to do with the level and the quality of the support and the style of the worker.

Social work support

Eleven of the young people and their families were currently receiving support from social workers from a local children and families team; six of these families were in Douglasshire. The availability of this kind of social work support was identified by a wide range of other professionals as a major issue in all three local authorities, where teams were hard pressed and had experienced major changes of staff. One young person in Glenmore Council had six social workers in a short space of time. Another family had valued the support of a student social worker but had been waiting for a year for a permanent replacement from the team. School staff, managers and Children's Reporters all identified a major issue of staff recruitment and stability amongst social workers in children and family teams where the main pressures were around child protection. However, in some cases young people and families valued the considerable individual support given by social workers whereas in one they were thought to be as much use as a 'chocolate fire guard' (Alan's aunt/carer).

Groupwork

Both young people and professionals often identified groupwork as an effective strategy for support. Sometimes groups were in-school, run jointly by a worker from a voluntary sector youth centre or from a local authority youth social work project with a guidance teacher. Groupwork was also a key feature of work in off site support units and neighbourhood based projects. Not only was this viewed very positively by the pupils who participated, but the joint working was also seen as developmental for the professional staff. Groupwork was offered to a small number of pupils, usually between five and twelve. It enables the exploring of problems with your peers in a safe group setting, facilitated by an adult or often two adults. Sometimes groups were composed of pupils, with quite different problems, sometimes with more specific referral criteria. These might include disruptiveness in class, low self-esteem, experience of being bullied, anger control or gender issues. The core conditions associated with counselling approaches are usually thought to apply to groupwork.

They involve active listening, offering unconditional positive regard, being genuine with pupils and of using empathy. Group leaders are expected to facilitate but not to direct the group and to be sensitive to the culture and process of the group as much as to the content of what is said. Often groups use games and exercises, especially role play and drama, as a strategy for helping pupils to relax and feel confident in exploring difficult issues.

> 'He is not a teacher, and he came into our group and I thought it would be different ... I thought it would be asking questions and telling us not to be bad, but instead he was just sitting down and playing games with us and getting us to think about our behaviour ... and I felt comfortable talking to him because [guidance teacher] was in that group as well.' *(Luke)*

Joint working like this was seen by staff to be helpful in breaking down barriers between professionals. For example, it reduced the suspicion of some teachers of the youth centre staff who dress more informally and use their first names with young people and, equally, external professionals increased their understanding of disciplinary issues in schools. Several teachers felt that their professional skills had been widened as a result of the joint working.

Specialist 'young people in difficulty' workers

Many of the young people in this group had also been involved at some point with staff in specialist 'youth social work' teams in Wallace City and Douglasshire. These teams often employed workers with a range of professional backgrounds, including education, social work and youth and community work. They offered intensive individual work and also groupwork with young people. Glenmore and Wallace City Councils also had part-time alternative education provision that was jointly funded by education and social work, offering services similar to that offered in the teams. Workers from these teams, along with those from neighbourhood voluntary youth projects, seemed often to be key members of the School Based Inter-agency Meetings and to be highly valued by young people and their families. They were also perceived as a valuable resource by school staff.

Educational psychologists

The role of the educational psychologists was, as stated earlier, mainly one of consultancy to the school staff, through regular more informal meetings with learning and behaviour support staff and guidance staff as well as in the School Based Inter-agency Meetings. The traditional educational psychologists' role of assessment and testing was still evident but was not so apparent in a more systems-based approach. They were involved more formally in assessment when this was required by procedures such as setting up a Record of Special Educational Needs or for referral to out of Council alternative educational provision. Referrals to the School Based Inter-agency Meetings did not necessarily involve a psychological assessment. However the young people with more complex difficulties were, in general, well known by the educational psychologists.

Individual work

Much of the work undertaken by different professionals with young people involved individual interviews, sometimes described simply as 'individual meetings' or 'individual work', sometimes as 'counselling'. There was some confusion, evident in this study, as in others, about what constitutes counselling and who can do it. Sometimes, although not often, the term was used to refer to formal counselling by a trained and supervised counsellor, at other times to denote an interview with a Guidance teacher. Sometimes individual interviews formed the basis of an assessment, reported to the School Based Inter-agency Meetings, sometimes they were the main form of support provided to some young people and were used to enable them to develop their own strategies, review progress or to talk through issues of current concern.

What was effective?

Figure 5.4 does suggest that on one level most of these pupils were not excluded in that they were no longer being formally excluded for disciplinary reasons but several of them had a rather limited involvement with school.

Figure 5.4 Pupils with complex problems: school position at time of interview

Braehead School (5 pupils)

- Out of school, half time in off campus support unit.
- Sometimes in school + outreach teaching.
- Left, transferred at own request to another school.
- In school, full-time normal timetable + extra help.
- Only occasionally in school.

Mooredge School (3 pupils)

- Out of school, full-time work focused project.
- In school, full-time normal timetable, still some truancy.
- In school, full-time normal timetable.

St Mary's School (1 pupil)

- In school, full-time normal timetable, still some truancy.

St John's School (1 pupil)

- In school, full-time normal timetable + groupwork.

Lochside School (2 pupils)

- In school, full-time + extraction with behaviour support teacher.
- In school, full-time normal timetable + extra help.

Benview School (2 pupils)

- Out of school, some tuition in library.
- In school, full-time normal timetable, still truancy.

'It must be working, I'm still here.' *(Colin)*

If the aim of inter-agency interventions is to keep pupils at least partly in their mainstream school, still connected with it, then the strategies in place could be seen to be effective for most of these pupils. However, if other criteria are used to denote success, such as full inclusion in school life and access to the full range of the curriculum then the picture becomes less clear. The connection with school for a number of those with complex patterns of difficulty was tenuous, they were the pupils for whom the school was clearly 'still trying'. Of the 11 of these young people who were still officially on the roll full time, several were still having real problems outwith school that affected their attendance. Others were still being occasionally excluded for a few days. In a few cases school staff regretted what they saw as failure. A guidance teacher said of Patrick, now in a full-time alternative work based project, 'We failed to keep him in school, even with intensive individual work.'

There was nonetheless a sense that the schools were really trying to hold on to these young people, not only because they were trying to reduce their exclusion figures but because they had a sense of the difficulties faced by the young people and a willingness to keep trying. Most of the young people in this group felt that some staff in their school were supportive, even when they were having conflict with others, particularly subject teachers. The parents of several young people, with significant difficulties in their families and their community, were kept in regular contact with the school through telephone calls. In one case where a young woman was sometimes absent and subject to violence from her brother she had an agreement to phone the assistant head teacher for help and advice.

Lindsay

The school supported Lindsay by placing her on a behaviour monitoring card and reducing her timetable to reduce her contact with other pupils (to avoid conflict/bullying). During this time Lindsay was excluded from school four times for verbal aggression and getting into fights, and it was agreed that she should attend the off site unit connected to the school and staffed by social work and teachers. Lindsay did well at this unit, responding to being in a smaller group and her attendance and aggression improved. This unit is only for those in second year and so Lindsay then moved to another small project jointly funded by social work and education. She enjoys attending this unit, describing it as a 'safe place' and saying that she has good friends here. The teachers and social workers in the unit describe Lindsay as more accepting of being challenged and less angry about things and she's more sociable.

There are still issues in the community, with Lindsay's mother describing how they come from a different area and are not accepted here. There have also been windows broken in the house and Lindsay continues to be involved in fights in the neighbourhood.

What was the inter-agency dimension to the support?

One major strength of the School Based Inter-agency Meetings was that, through information sharing by various professionals, the school staff had a strong sense of the range of problems being faced by some of these pupils out of school and were therefore more willing to continue to keep trying. This highlights a major contribution of the meetings which promoted an understanding of the complex and sometimes very distressing outside world of children's lives. In addition the combined professional knowledge of the different professionals enabled a creative and imaginative approach to addressing problems. The support from colleagues of other professions was valued by school staff, particularly when the school was holding onto very challenging young people and there was pressure from other school staff to exclude. The meetings offered an opportunity, when a plan did not seem to be working or to need additional dimensions, to develop other strategies or identify further resources.

Discussion of all four groups

A varying range of agencies

The nature and level of support provided to individual young people, and sometimes to their families, varied considerably between local authorities, schools and young people. Predictably those young people identified as having a complex range of problems were more likely to have been involved with a range of support services beyond those available in school. The support specified often reflected the character of the resources available to the school, for example in Douglasshire most provision was provided through the local authority's own services whereas in the other two local authorities considerable use was made of voluntary sector projects, which are partly 'arm's length' funded by the local authority. Availability of resources was also affected by the characteristics of the local authorities, as discussed in earlier chapters. Wallace City Council is a city with some very disadvantaged housing areas, so resources were available to Braehead School partly through those concentrated in the neighbourhood and partly from a range of city-wide schemes. Both Glenmore and Douglasshire were affected by the distances between centres where some resources were located.

Effective helpers

'Well there was this woman once who helped.' *(Kelly)*

When asked about what makes an effective helper both parents and young people appeared unequivocal – it is about being listened too, respected and treated fairly. Often they did not know the professional status of professionals they had been involved with. Young people and families were particularly responsive to those who approached them in an open, collaborative, non-judgemental way. Although these features cannot be attributable to any particular profession, it seemed that the informal style of the workers from the voluntary agencies and the specialist youth social work teams, which combined information, advice and counselling skills in an everyday conversational manner, made it easy for parent and young people to respond positively to them.

'Before the summer I went to the [youth centre]. We went on trips and everything. If something happened, you could speak to them about it and they wouldn't shout at you or anything.' *(Kylie)*

This informal style with young people was often combined, in the role of these professionals, with a quite focused approach to addressing particular issues in young people's lives, often using individual counselling approaches or groupwork as part of a clearly defined strategy with defined aims. Most also seemed to record and to evaluate their work on a regular basis, communicating this with other professionals. A further strength of three of the voluntary sector youth projects which were highly valued was that their context was that of a neighbourhood youth centre offering open youth club provision as well as some highly specialised support services, so there was no stigma in being involved with them.

Support by unqualified workers

Some valued support was provided by workers with no formal qualifications, such as volunteers, befrienders, sessional workers from youth centres or from a family support team and classroom auxiliaries or learning support assistants. There were issues raised by some professionals about the level of training and supervision provided for these workers. One parent gave an example of an auxiliary cutting her daughter's hair in class without asking for permission. Others however valued the down to earth approach to people who may be from the same neighbourhood or perceived to share the same culture.

The theoretical bases of the work with young people

Much of the work described by professionals and by young people did not seem to be based in particular theoretical perspectives or models of practice, other than that developed informally through the individual professional's own knowledge and experience. The discussion in the School Based Inter-agency Meetings reflected an awareness of recent thinking about child development and about risk factors in children's lives. In individual practice with young people broadly person-centred models of counselling skills were often combined with some structured exercises derived from cognitive behavioural approaches. Social groupwork approaches emphasising personal growth and development and relationship building were also often combined with social skills exercises, role play, drama and games in an eclectically based approach which was perhaps typical of how the Scottish approach to groupwork with young people has developed. Educational psychologists were more likely to suggest a particular focus for their work, broadly social constructivist in outlook, reflecting the shift mentioned earlier from individually focused work to a more consultative role in relation to the systems in which they work.

Evaluation and monitoring

There was not always a sufficiently detailed and clear recording of aims, desired outcomes and evaluations. Often the absence of disruptiveness may simply be assumed to be the desired outcome. Records held in school and by different professionals were varied in their quality. Perhaps the most clear and comprehensive were those developed by the specialist workers in the youth social work teams and the voluntary youth agencies. Formal social work and school records sometimes reflected how busy the staff were and were disorganised and often did not contain a clear history of strategies used or of professionals involved. The specialist workers were also the most likely to have written formal evaluations of their work, including comments from young people. This of course sometimes was easier for those workers who were engaged in bounded and focused pieces of work. School staff, in particular, seemed to be constantly busy with the day to day managing of the face to face work with young people and with colleagues, particularly in relation to those with the most complex difficulties. Time for reflection and evaluation was scarce.

Conclusion

What follows is a summary of findings in relation to effectiveness both in terms of preventing exclusion from school and in terms of the subjective views of participants about support:

- **There were things that 'worked' but there is no single answer.** The strategies varied and could not be predicted to work for all pupils.

- **Support strategies for young people with less complex difficulties were often not that different from those provided for the young people with more complex difficulties.** However, they were more likely to have been a one-off intervention and more often regarded as successful.

- **Some things work for some pupils in some places and some times.** Most of the young people were helped, both in terms of avoiding and reducing exclusion and in terms of coping better with difficulties outside school.

- **The right help at the right time.** When intervention or support was helpful it was seen by young people to have been what made sense for them at that time in their life. Sometimes what might seem to be appropriate by professionals does not work because of other factors in young people's lives.

- **Professional plans were most effective when they were responsive to individual circumstances.** The most effective support was not about a matching of perceived problems with a standard model of support; instead it took account of the wishes and the life circumstances of the young people.

- **The voice of the young people was not always strongly heard however.** The question of real participation in decision making was raised in the previous chapter. Equally the place of young people in planning and evaluating was patchy; sometimes they felt clearly involved, but others felt themselves to be the subject of professional intervention.

- **Sometimes it only took one person.** Effective support was sometimes a matter of one person providing some additional help for a short time or in quite an informal style. Some young people appreciated the willingness of certain professionals to take an advocacy role.

- **The manner or style of support was important to young people and families.** Often the style or manner in which the support was offered affected how it was received. If the professional was perceived as non-judgemental, equitable and genuine in the process then it was more likely to have been experienced as effective.

- **An informal style was particularly regarded as effective when combined with an organised programme of support.** Many professionals also valued the work of colleagues who combined a warm, informal supportive style in structured programmes with clearly defined aims for their work with individual young people.

- **Keeping in touch.** Just keeping in touch and maintaining contact with some young people was important in supporting them in school or in encouraging them to return to school.

- **Hanging on in there/still trying.** A combination of persistence and flexibility was very important in supporting young people with complex difficulties. Recognising the interrelated nature of such difficulties means that schools had to keep 'hanging on in there' even when it was difficult to be optimistic.

- **High maintenance pupils.** Schools and local authorities recognised that some such pupils may continue to need a high level of support, and short-term programmes designed to 'solve' problems may not be effective immediately. They may however operate as a platform for further support.

- **Being a problem was not seen as the same as having a problem.** While school and other staff did emphasise the need to address issues of disruption it was helpful if a clear distinction was understood between strategies to improve school behaviour and those aimed at supporting individual pupils. Some pupils in this study benefited from both.

- **It was not easy.** Many staff talked of how difficult they felt it was sometimes to find the right strategy and to keep trying. In some cases there was agreement amongst professionals that an out of school placement was the only option for a young person, even when that was not always wished by the pupils or parent. In some cases the school staff did feel that they had failed.

6. Summary and conclusions

'I like the fact that they're trying to keep them in the school, they're trying.'
(Donald's mother, Mooredge School)

This study explored issues of effectiveness in inter-agency working in preventing school exclusion in Scotland. This chapter summarises the findings. It outlines the national and local context for inter-agency working, focusing on the three local authorities and six schools in the study. It looks at effectiveness in preventing exclusion, particularly in relation to School Based Inter-agency Meetings and strategies developed to support individual young people.

The context of inter-agency working in three Scottish local authorities

The study has been timely in the context of a range of initiatives at government level, both north and south of the border. These have emphasised social inclusion and joined-up working. Reduction of disciplinary exclusion from school has been a key plank of these initiatives. At the same time Ministers in both Scotland and England have responded sympathetically to concerns from head teachers and teachers about school discipline.

There are certain features of the policy and practice landscape in Scotland relevant to making sense of our findings. These include:

- A long history of inter-agency working in Scottish local authorities.
- The welfare based approach of the Scottish Children's Hearing System.
- The Children Act (Scotland) 1995, its definitions of need and right to involvement in decision making.
- The New Community schools pilot programme, emphasising joined-up work.
- The Standards in Scotland's Schools etc Act 2000, providing the right to schooling and the presumption of mainstream school.

- Differences from other parts of Britain in policy and practice on disciplinary exclusion, lower rates and national Guidance emphasis on inclusion, but still concerns over numbers excluded.
- A stronger role of local authorities in policy development, no opted out schools, a commitment to the idea of the comprehensive school.
- A broad model of difficulties in learning and SEN, including the idea of social, emotional and behavioural difficulties.

There are aspects of the Scottish approach to education and social welfare, which may be important in understanding these findings. Some of the above may be seen as distinctively different, others may be viewed more as a Scottish slant on a common British issue and there clearly are features and issues in common.

- A complex and not joined-up policy context.
- Tensions between policy and practice over (S)EBD and SEN and their relationship with exclusion.
- Rights to participation in decision making different in social welfare, juvenile justice and educational structures.
- Exclusion statistics reflect varying practices between local authorities and schools.
- Rapid policy innovation and considerable short-term funding.

The three local authorities

- Each local authority had a history of inter-agency working; these were still evolving and changing in response to local authority restructuring and policy developments. The local authorities varied considerably, in terms of their geographic, demographic, social and economic characteristics.
- Douglasshire, the Council with the highest level of unemployment in Scotland, had the highest rate of exclusion from school of the three, although by no means the highest in Scotland. Wallace City had the highest rate of school absence of the three local authorities. Glenmore Council had the highest rates of recorded school attainment, the other two were very close to the national average.
- Services to young people in difficulty were more likely to be delivered by a mixture of local authority and voluntary sector provision in Wallace City and Glenmore but were more likely to be local authority managed in Douglasshire. The nature and level of services available to individual young people, and their families, varied considerably between local authorities, schools and young people. All three local authorities had policies of educational inclusion but continued to place some pupils in special day and residential provision.

- Social work and education in Douglasshire had been merged into one department. In all local authorities there were issues about staff pressures, retention and recruitment of staff in children and family social work teams.
- Each local authority had written policies about working together to support vulnerable pupils and to prevent disciplinary exclusion. School Based Inter-agency Meetings were a key element of policy and practice in all three local authorities.

School Based Inter-agency Meetings: differences and similarities between local authorities

- Remits for School Based Inter-agency Meetings in Douglasshire and Wallace City focused on a broad range of difficulties faced by pupils. These included difficulties in learning, special educational needs leading to Records, and other concerns in addition to exclusion.
- Glenmore had a multi-stranded staged approach to support for learning. In this study we looked at the strand of School Based Inter-agency Meetings particularly focused on SEBD and exclusion. The meetings in Douglasshire were case based. The meetings in the other two local authorities were combined case/strategic.
- In all three local authorities the meetings were a necessary stage in accessing out of school or out of local authority resources. Schools were expected in all three local authorities to demonstrate that they had tried a range of strategies before referring to meetings. Douglasshire Council had two levels of School Based Inter-agency Meetings, the first intended to explore fully the range of strategies available through existing resources, the second to discuss access to wider resources. In the other two local authorities these aspects were addressed in the same meetings, but could be referred on to local authority-wide meetings.

The schools

- The six schools were all quite different. They were all however considered by their local authorities to be developing effective inter-agency work in preventing exclusion. Their populations varied considerably in terms of economic and social disadvantage. The two schools with the highest level of eligibility to free school meals also had the highest rates of exclusion in 1999/2000. However, St Mary's and St John's with similar levels of eligibility, had very different rates of exclusion. St John's School had the lowest rate of exclusion in the study.

- Very few pupils were excluded without readmission to the register from the schools, four from St John's, one from Braehead. There were no systematic differences between the schools in terms of the range of support offered to young people, other than those indicated as differences in the range of services available in their local authorities.

- Differences in the rates of exclusion probably reflected wider differences in the schools and in their use of exclusion. Schools in Douglasshire seemed more likely to use exclusion as a more routine disciplinary sanction, rather than always as a last resort.

The young people

- The 30 young people interviewed were selected by their schools as examples of effective inter-agency working. They fell into three groups; a fourth and largest group (Group 1) was also identified who were excluded and discussed at the School Based Inter-agency Meetings but where a school only response was necessary.

- Group 2 were 12 pupils who may have been excluded only once, perhaps unexpectedly for something quite serious or those with some persistent difficulties in school but who were not thought to have a significant range of major problems outside school.

- Group 3 were four pupils with Records of Special Educational Needs, three of whom had diagnosed conditions thought to underlie their school difficulties.

- Group 4 were 14 young people with multiple and complex difficulties in their lives, in school and in their families and in their neighbourhoods.

School Based Inter-agency Meetings

- The meetings varied significantly in terms of the focus of the meetings and in terms of whether there was participation of young people and/or parents. They also varied in the number, occupation and status of professional staff attending. Variations in attendance partly reflected whether the meetings were case based, in where only relevant professionals attended, or combined case/strategic, where there was a wider permanent membership in addition to professionals relevant for individual young people.

- There was an issue in both local authorities about regular attendance of some professionals, especially under pressure social workers. Mental health staff tended not to participate. Everyone interviewed felt that meetings were most effective when all relevant professionals participated.

- Young people and their parents/carers participated in the School Based Inter-agency Meetings in Douglasshire. They valued their participation, although they did not always understand all aspects and sometimes found them intimidating or upsetting. In the other two local authorities pupils and parents often met with a sub-group of staff before or after meetings. Some felt they would prefer to be at the wider meetings, others said that they would find it uncomfortable. Several young people were not clear about what had been discussed.

- Case based meetings increased involvement by young people and parents/carers. Combined case/strategic meetings discussed and planned wider service delivery in relation to vulnerable young people and young people with SEBD. They had a permanent core membership with a history of working together. There were clear advantages to the combined meetings in the positive working relationships of the members, their ability to be imaginative and creative in both case based and more strategic thinking. There were issues of confidentiality when young people were discussed in case/strategic meetings when professionals not directly involved were present. However, in meetings observed, such professionals often made helpful suggestions or offers of support.

- All School Based Inter-agency Meetings discussed problems, assessed the current circumstances of pupils' lives, made plans, revising and reviewing them when necessary. There was limited evidence of systematic evaluation of the outcomes of the meetings, other than through the review of individual cases. All professional staff interviewed felt that the School Based Inter-agency Meetings were central to their work and felt that the *joint* working in the meetings did promote a *joined-up* view of pupils' lives.

- Criticisms were identified by some staff over resources available to meetings and the patchy attendance of some colleagues. Some school staff felt that the problems were sometimes pushed back onto the school, whereas some other professionals felt that they were expected to solve the problems of the school. Although it was clear that the School Based Inter-agency Meetings had increased awareness of the roles and responsibilities of other professionals, sometimes under pressure old loyalties and differences of professionals' judgement were still barriers to effective work.

- The meetings did take a great deal of professional time, not only in the meetings but in related activities of assessing, sub-meetings of professionals, sometimes with young people and parents, recording and communication around matters for and from meetings.

Did the inter-agency work studied prevent exclusion and provide support?

- Most of the case study pupils were being maintained in mainstream school, at least part time but in a few cases the connection was tenuous. Two pupils were in full-time alternative provision, two others in part-time alternative provision. One was still mainly excluded, receiving some part-time tuition. Pupils still in mainstream were not all fully included into the curriculum.

- There were a range of effective strategies used to maintain young people in school. They tended to include quite a high level of support from school staff, before and during intervention from other professionals. They were mainly based on a view of the young person as in need of support, rather than as a response to disciplinary exclusion. The strategies varied and could not be predicted to be effective for all pupils.

- Plans and strategies worked when they were the right thing for the young person at that time. They were individualised, taking account of individual life circumstances and were based in a joined-up knowledge of a range of approaches.

- The wishes and opinions of young people and their families were sometimes but not always a key feature of support plans.

- The style and manner of support was important to young people and parents/carers interviewed. Support offered by professionals was valued when it was perceived as non-judgemental, genuine and equitable. Professionals and families valued the support provided by those staff with a specialised focus on vulnerable young people, particularly those in youth social work teams and in voluntary sector projects. Their strength seemed to be in the combination of a warm, informal, non-judgemental style with clearly structured aims and evaluation of programmes.

- Some of the young people in this study had been involved with a range of support agencies and were still very challenging in school. Most professionals made the point that a few pupils required a level of 'high maintenance' in school. Supporting the pupils with complex and multiple difficulties was not easy and seemed to be a matter of 'hanging on in there', of keeping trying and not giving up. All the pupils in this study felt that there had been someone in their own school who was on their side.

Figure 6.1 Contribution of inter-agency working to effective support

Inter-agency work contributed by:

- Providing a joined-up, child-centred perspective on young people's lives.
- Offering a supportive forum for staff to exchange views and generate ideas.
- Widening awareness of other strategies and outside school resources.
- Assessing and planning for individual needs.
- Reviewing and revising plans and developing additional or different approaches.
- Providing an avenue to out of school provision.
- Supporting school staff in challenging school management or colleagues over issues of exclusion.
- Planning the contribution of a range of professionals.
- Responsiveness of professionals to the views and experiences of young people.

Several professionals talked of the expensive use of professional time in the School Based Inter-agency Meetings. Figure 6.2 lists those features that appeared to characterise successful meetings.

Figure 6.2 Features of effective meetings

General features

- A clear remit.
- Specified aims and objectives.
- An appropriate place.
- All relevant professionals attend.
- A warm climate of welcome for participants.
- An opportunity for all participants to be involved.
- Sensitivity to those who find participation difficult.
- A clear policy/understanding about confidentiality and the disclosure of information.
- A non-punitive approach to young people.
- Focus on strategies not histories.
- Knowledge of resources currently available.
- A history of working together.
- Some consistency of membership.
- Minutes are clear and accessible.
- Decisions are reviewed.
- Regular evaluation both of outcomes of decisions and of the meetings themselves.

Case based

- Professionals all known to the young person and family.
- Good clear information about purposes of meeting.

(continued)

- Information about rights to participation in decision making.
- Language used is clear and jargon free.
- Decisions are understood by all participants.
- Structure for clear recording and timetable for evaluation of plans for supporting young people.
- Outcomes of the meeting are clearly recorded.

Practice in legislative and policy contexts

We suggested earlier that the policy context for the work involved in preventing or establishing alternatives to exclusion is confusing. The work explored in this study involves professionals trying to collaborate in relation to legislation and policy which is not joined-up at national level. It is clear from interviews in this project with young people, families *and* professionals that many do not have a comprehensive picture of the rights and responsibilities of families or of professionals, as specified in the rather different laws and procedures. At local authority level the changing policies and associated procedures on exclusion, pupil support and inter-agency working, as well as those associated with the Social Work Departments and the Children's Hearing System, are difficult to understand even for the professionals involved in these complex systems, but even more so for those on the periphery like class and subject teachers. Rapid policy innovation and short-term funding of projects also contribute to a sense of it being difficult to keep up with developments.

Policies on School Based Inter-agency Meetings in the three local authorities referred to pupils who may be seen to require additional support in school in terms of their social and emotional development, not only those who were disruptive or at risk of exclusion. This model is consistent with a view that does not separate the 'bad' from the 'worthy' and that recognises the frequent interaction between difficulties in learning and disruption and disaffection. It therefore offers a possible route into more inclusive schooling but also does allow for strategies to be employed which exclude in a wider sense – the policies and structures which governed the operation of the School Based Inter-agency Meetings place these meetings in a system that also allows for a route out of the mainstream and into more specialised provision. The existence of policies of inclusion and of reducing exclusion co-exist in a context which emphasises standards of school attainment and allows for the continued removal of pupils seen to threaten this.

One clear advantage of the inter-agency working described in this study was that it led to a broad holistic view of young people's lives: they were not seen simply as discipline problems. The reverse of this is that sometimes schools may view classroom management problems in terms of an individualised model of a pupil's difficulties, rather than exploring aspects of the pedagogy, the curriculum or specific classroom management techniques of teachers. Perhaps sometimes the purpose of the communication between professionals is to recognise when a problem should continue to belong to the school.

Not just matching resources to problems – the key is the young person's voice

The findings from this study suggest that there are a range of effective ways of supporting young people at risk of disciplinary exclusion and that there were things that worked for particular young people but there are no simple answers. Some of the things that worked were to do with the skills and the characteristics of the workers, sometimes they were because they were at the right time in a young person's life and sometimes they worked because everyone just kept trying, 'still hanging on in there' (assistant head teacher, Braehead). Plans or strategies worked when they were the right thing for the young person at that time – when they were individualised responses.

Professional staff were knowledgeable about a range of possible approaches and possible resources. This could never however be a simple matter of matching resources to problems as it was clear that the history and preferences of individual young people made this unrealistic. Thus the involvement of the young people and their families is central to the process both in order to protect their rights and to ensure that effective strategies can be developed to avoid the potentially damaging consequences of school exclusion.

References

Arblaster, L and others (1999) *Achieving the Impossible. Interagency collaboration to address the housing, health and social care needs of people able to live in ordinary housing.* Policy Press

Closs, A 'Special educational provision' *in* Clark, M M and Munn, P eds (1997) *Education in Scotland, Policy and Practice from Pre-school to Secondary.* Routledge

Cohen, R and others (1994) *School's Out: The Family Perspective on School Exclusion.* Family Service Unit and Barnados

Farrell, K and Tsakalidou, K (1999) *Recent trends in the re-integration of pupils with emotional and behavioural difficulties in the United Kingdom.* Research Report, University of Manchester

Hill, M. (1999) 'What's the problem? Who can help?' The perspective of children and young people on their well-being and on helping professionals, *Journal of Social Work Practice*, 13, 2, 135–45

HM Inspector of Schools (HMI) (2001) *Alternatives to school exclusion.* HMI

Kendrick, A 'Supporting families through inter-agency work: youth strategies' *in* Hill, M, Kirk, R and Part, D eds (1995) *Supporting Families.* HMSO

Kendrick, A, Simpson, M and Mapstone, E (1996) *Getting it together: Changing services for children and young people in difficulty.* Joseph Rowntree Foundation

Leathard, A ed. (1994) *Going Inter-Professional. Working Together for Health and Welfare.* Routledge

Lloyd, G and Padfield, P (1996) Re-integration into Mainstream. Gi'e us peace, *British Journal of Special Education*, 23, 4, 180–86

Munn, P, Lloyd, G and Cullen, M (2000) *Alternatives to Exclusion from School.* Paul Chapman

Parsons, C (1999) *Education, Exclusion and Citizenship*. Routledge

Parsons, C 'The Third Way to educational and social exclusion' *in* Walraven, G and others *eds* (2000) *Combating Social Exclusion through Education.* Leuven-Appeldoorn: Garant

Paterson, L 'Policy making in Scottish education: a case of pragmatic nationalism' *in* Clark, M and Munn, P *eds* (1997) *Education in Scotland: policy and practice from pre-school to secondary.* Routledge

Pickles, T 'Youth strategies in Scotland' *in* Lloyd, G *ed.* (1992) *Chosen with Care? Responses to Disturbing and Disruptive Behaviour.* Moray House Publications

Schaffer, M 'Children's Hearings and school problems' *in* Lloyd, G *ed.* (1992) *Chosen with Care? Responses to Disturbing and Disruptive Behaviour.* Moray House Publications

Scottish Executive (1998) *New Community Schools Prospectus* (www.scotland.gov.uk/library/documents-w3/ncsp-00.htm) Accessed November 2000

Scottish Executive (1999) *Making it happen.* Report of the Strategy Action Team (http:www.scotland.gov.uk/inclusion/docs/maih-oo.htm) Accessed November 2000

Scottish Executive (2000a) *Draft Guidance on Presumption of Inclusion in Standards in Scottish Schools etc 2000.*

Scottish Executive (2000b) *Exclusions from Schools, 1998/99.* Press Release.

Scottish Executive (2000c) *Leavers' Destinations from Scottish Secondary Schools 1996/97 to 1998/99.*

Scottish Executive (2000d) *Examination results in Scottish Schools.*

Scottish Executive (2001a) *Exclusions from Schools, 1999/2000.* Press Release

Scottish Executive (2001b) *Children Looked After in the Year to 31 March 2000.*

Scottish Executive (2001c) *School Meals in Education Authority Schools 1999/2000.*

Scottish Executive (2001d) *Attendance and Absence in Scottish Schools 1999/2000.*

Scottish Office (1964) *The Kilbrandon Report.* HMSO

Scottish Office (1993) *Scotland's Children,* White Paper. HMSO

Scottish Office (1997) *Scotland's Children: The Children (Scotland) Act 1995 Regulations and Guidance*

Scottish Office (1998) *Guidance on Issues Concerning Exclusion from School.* Circular No 2/98

Scottish Office (1998) *Alternatives to Exclusion Grant Scheme, Specification for Bids*

Scottish Office Education and Industry Department (SOEID) (1996) *Children and Young Persons with Special Educational Needs: Assessment and Recording.* Circular 4/96

Triseliotis, J and others (1995) *Teenagers and the social work services.* HMSO

Wilson, V and Pirrie, A (2000) *Multidisciplinary Teamworking: Beyond the Barriers? A Review of the Issues.* Scottish Executive

Index